AMERICAN FOLK ART

WILLIAM C. KETCHUM, JR.

ABOUT THE AUTHOR

WILLIAM KETCHUM is the author of over thirty books and numerous magazine articles on American antiques and collectibles. A former attorney, Mr. Ketchum has been a professor, lecturer, and guest curator for more than twenty years at such institutions as the Smithsonian, the New School for Social Research, and New York University. He is currently very active at the Museum of American Folk Art in New York City, where he is a member of both the International Advisory Committee and the faculty of the Folk Art Institute. Mr. Ketchum presently resides in Rye, New York.

MASON CREST

MASON CREST
450 Parkway Drive, Suite D
Broomall, Pennsylvania 19008
(866) MCP-BOOK (toll free)

Printed and bound in the United States of America.

First printing
1 3 5 7 9 8 6 4 2

ISBN (hardback) 978-1-4222-3932-2
ISBN (series) 978-1-4222-3930-8
ISBN (ebook) 978-1-4222-7854-3

Cataloging-in-Publication Data on file
with the Library of Congress

PICTURE CREDITS

12 (left), 24-25, 27 (bottom), 31 (top), 35, 42 (top), 48, 61,
(left & right), 64, 68, 69 (top), 72, (left), 75, 79, 81, 85 (top),
88-89, 94, 96, 103, 104, 110, 112-113, 114 (left),
118, 120-121, 122, 123 (top & bottom),
124-125, 126, 127, 128, 129, 130 (right), 134, 135, 140, 142 (top)
All pages above: Schecter Lee/ESTO

30, 32, 34 (top), 40-41, 130 (left),
132, 136-137, 139, 142 (bottom), 143
All pages above: Chun Y. Lai/ESTO

85 (bottom) supplied by the Museum of American Folk Art,
New York City

FRONT COVER PHOTOGRAPH BY
Esto Photographies

BACK COVER PHOTOGRAPH BY
Schecter Lee/Esto Photographics

Cover design by Mark Weinberg

FOLK ART—THE ART OF THE COMMON MAN—

is as much a part of the American way of life as baseball and apple pie. Since the time of the earliest settlers, Americans—professionals and amateurs alike— have been expressing their individuality through the creation and embellishment of everyday objects. From furniture and kitchen utensils to weathervanes and shop signs, folk art has come to be synonymous with the art of inclusion. In this beautifully illustrated volume, noted author and curator William Ketchum explores our glorious folk-art heritage in all its simple splendor.

Beginning with that most basic American institution, the family, this book investigates the varied arts of home and community. Before the invention of the camera, portraiture—not just the province of the wealthy—was practiced in the forms of painting and silhouette cutting; domestic and regional scenes were also memorialized on canvas in genre paintings. The departed, too, were remembered in the arts of mourning pictures and gravestone carving.

Folk art often appeared in many other guises around the house. Lovingly hand-crafted wooden objects from kitchenware to furniture were produced in great profusion, as were metal pieces such as doorstops and hitching posts. The religious paintings and carvings of the Southwest were also a popular expression of homely values. All of these and more are illustrated in these pages in some of the most intriguing examples of their types.

In Victorian times particularly, folk art was often created in the pursuit of many different hobbies, practiced both as solitary occupations and in the context of social gatherings. It was through these avocations that such prized collectibles as theorem paintings, whimsies, and tramp art were fashioned. Beautifully flourished calligraphy, complex reverse paintings on glass, and intricately carved walking sticks are also pictured here, along with evocative descriptions of the traditions which gave rise to these art forms.

Outside the home weathervanes were a common item, a craft which, like so many folk arts, was both practical and decorative. With a history reaching back to ancient times, these were produced in an astonishing variety of shapes, from the ubiquitous rooster to the familiar Uncle Sam. Whirligigs, too, were a favorite windblown sculpture, serving primarily as an amusement for both young and old.

Folk art was found in many forms around the town as well. Chapter Five explores these public crafts, which are some of the most sought-after by today's collectors and museums. Architectural elements, shop signs, tobacconists' figures, and carousel animals are all pictured here, with fascinating commentary on their histories and modern expressions.

More than any other group of people, sailors were responsible for the creation of an enormous range of folk arts. In this next chapter, the author presents nautical art in its myriad forms; scrimshaw, ship models and paintings, rope work, and ship carvings are but a few described and illustrated here.

Finally, the world of miniatures is explored, in all its charming detail. From eminently useful duck decoys to purely ornamental ceramic mantel figurines, miniatures have long been a favored handiwork in American homes. Stone and chalkware pieces are discussed as well, along with the more recent "wacky wood," a souvenir with which every tourist is familiar.

An integral part of our American culture and history, folk art is a fascinating and wide-ranging topic. This book, with its stunning illustrations' and engrossing commentary, will prove an invaluable addition to the library of any collector or enthusiast.

CONTENTS

INTRODUCTION

F olk art, the art of the "common man" (as opposed to the formal art commissioned and appreciated by the wealthy and well-educated), is by no means unique to the United States. However, it is here that it thrived, encouraged by the emergence of the world's first sizable middle class and a nearly universal belief that art, like all else, should be open and available to everyone.

This belief encouraged the proliferation during the 18th and 19th centuries of a group of carvers and painters whose range of skills differed substantially from that of their European counterparts. Many had no formal artistic training, and in their failure to follow traditional rules of perspective, proportion, and color blending they produced an abstract style which often seems shockingly modern to 20th-century eyes.

Moreover, unlike the European academics, they were jacks-of-all-trades. American portrait painters also regularly painted wagons, coaches, tavern signs, or even houses. Sculptors shifted readily from classical human forms to tobacconists' figures and ships' figureheads. In a widespread and sparsely settled society, each man (or woman) did what was required.

Much of this work was certainly not viewed by its creators or consumers as "art." Indeed, most of them adhered to the same traditional view held by their self-anointed social and economic superiors: "art" was limited to Greek and Roman sculpture, academic paintings, bronzes, prints, engravings, and the like. What they produced, on the other hand, was what was needed by their emerging communities.

It is writers, museum curators, collectors, and antique dealers who have, in this century, defined (and continue to define) these practical objects as folk art. The earliest folk art collectors, themselves artists or wealthy art patrons, were drawn to what they knew, traditional painting and sculpture. Others, more sensitive to the broader definitions of these mediums, discovered the folk-art qualities of such utilitarian items as weathervanes, shop signs, carved utensils, and figural ceramics.

Today, as reflected in this book, such diverse objects as factory-made cast iron doorstops, architectural fragments, and molded carnival chalkware are embraced as folk art. There is no reason to believe that the process of inclusion will be reversed. New items or categories (such as "wacky wood") are continually being embraced; nothing once included is later rejected. This, too, is part of the American way. As the more traditional folk forms have been priced out of most collectors' range, tastemakers and dealers have obligingly discovered new and less costly types or, as with 20th-century folk art, a whole century of new material. All, in the belief, of course, that "art, like all else, should be open and available to everyone."

BIRTH AND BAPTISMAL CERTIFICATE c. 1806; watercolor on paper fractur, attributed to Barbara Becker Haman (b.1774), Shennadoah County, Virginia. Related to European illuminated manuscripts, fractur drawings were created primarily by American aritsts of Germanic background. *Courtesy Sotheby's.*

Die liebe Sonne
Scheint für alle

Geburts und   Tauf=Schein.

Diesen beyden Ehegatten als Johañes Daman
und seiner ehelichen Hausfrau Barbara eine geborene
Beckerin wurde ein Sohn Zur Welt geboren
im Jahr unsers Herrn 1806. den 29=ten Tag
Monats August. dieser Sohn ist geboren in
Shenandoa County im Staat Virginia
in Nord America. und erhielt bey der
heiligen Taufe den Namen Elias, den
21=7bris 1806. von Herrn
Pfarrer   Hoffman
die TaufZeug waren Joh:
Georg Hottel und
. . . . .

CHAPTER 1

REMEMBERING
THE FAMILY

Folk art is, above all else, family art, carried out in a variety of mediums and with a multitude of purposes. Oil and watercolor portraits, silhouettes, memorial paintings, and gravestone art serve to perpetuate the memory of the living and the dead, while their surroundings, homes, and community are preserved through genre or "memory" painting. As with most folk art, the creators might have been professionals working for a fee or talented amateurs creating for their own satisfaction.

Portraits

It is difficult for us, in this age of still and video cameras and home movies, to imagine the importance of the portrait artist in memorializing the family. Yet until 1839, when Louis Jacques Mande' Daguerre (1787-1851) invented the daguerreotype, only the artist and the silhouette cutter could render a likeness.

Portrait painting had in Europe long been the prerogative of the royal and the rich; in the American colonies those who could afford it had their likenesses painted by academy-trained artists, usually of English origin. However, this was a "New World" with new ideas. The rising merchant, artisan, and farmer classes also wanted portraits, and if they could not afford the best professionals, they could afford home-grown portraitists. These might not have been academy-trained, but they were professionals in that they worked for a fee.

Referred to as limners (from the French *luminare*, to light up or illuminate, as in the fraktur decorations which embellished early religious tracts), these artists worked in both city and country. In fact, many spent their winters in large cities like New York or Baltimore and their summers wandering from town to town across the countryside. Typically, they would take rooms at the local inn or board with a farmer (often paying with a family portrait) and would advertise for patrons in the local paper.

PORTRAIT OF A YOUNG WOMAN c. 1830-1850; oil on canvas; attributed to William Matthew Prior (1806-1873), active in Maine and Massachusetts. Images of children are among the most popular of all folk art subjects. *Private Collection.*

PORTRAIT OF A YOUNG WOMAN c. 1825-1840; watercolor on paper; attributed to J. Evans, New Hampshire. Background details enhance the worth of this charming picture. *Author's Collection.*

Following Page:
WATERMELON PARTY 1975; oil on canvas; by Mattie Lou O'Kelley (1908-), Maysville, Georgia. O'Kelley, who created this genre painting, is one of the best known 20th century folk artists and has documented life in the rural South. *Private Collection.*

These ads, like the one placed by George Mason in the *Boston News-Letter* of January 7, 17◖ often reflected the artist's sensitivity to the economic realities of his profession:

> **GEORGE MASON, Limner, begs leave to inform the Public That (with a view to more constant Employ) he now draws Faces in Crayons for Two Guineas each, Glass and Frame included, as the above-mentioned Terms are extremely moderate, he flatters himself with meeting some Encouragement.**

Indeed, it was not unusual for the portrait painter to offer several grades of work, ranging fr◖ a fully-developed piece with extensive background details, to what was little more than a bare c◖ ored outline of the sitter. The New England artist Matthew Prior (1806-1873) noted in his adv◖ tising that "persons wishing for a flat picture can have a likeness without shade or shadow at ◖ quarter price."

Although they seldom had much professional training, these itinerant artists often develop◖ high degrees of facility and idiosyncratic styles which must have appealed to their custom◖ (some produced hundreds of paintings) and certainly appeals to the contemporary collect◖ Though often lacking in techniques such as the use of shading or spatial relationships, th◖ were skilled at hiding their shortcomings (hard-to-render hands and ears would be conceal◖ within vests or beneath hats) and maximizing their strengths, such as the ability to exec◖ elaborate decorative details.

Since many also worked as sign, coach, wall painters, these artist-craftsmen gloried◖ planes of bold, flat colors and the jewel-l◖ details of earrings, hair combs, and shaw◖ Customers admiring the rich sheen of a n◖ green velvet dress or the status reflected the presence in the portrait of a newspaper◖ bible (it meant the sitter could read!) we◖ likely to overlook slightly misplaced featur◖

Moreover, despite any defects in their ov◖ technique the limners were much aware◖ the academic art world. They employed◖ forms English portrait prints or "heads" a◖ regularly perused how-to books such as *T◖ School of Wisdom or Repository of the M◖ Valuable Curiosities of Art*, published in Ne◖ Brunswick, New Jersey in 1787.

This did not, however, always help. T◖ revealingly frank diary of the artist Jam◖ Guild (1797-1844) notes that on the way◖ Bloomfield, New York he

> put up at a tavern and told a Young Lady that if she would wash my shirt, I would draw her likeness....The poor Girl sat niped up so prim and looked so smileing...while I was daubing on a piece of paper, it could not be called painting, for it looked more like a strangle cat than it did like her. However, I told her it looked like her and she believed it.

PORTRAIT OF
ARCHER PAYNE, JR. c. 1791; oil on canvas; attributed to the Payne Limner, Virginia. The use here of guns, dogs, and hunting trophies reflects the mannerisms of traditional English portraiture. *Courtesy Sotheby's.*

**PORTRAIT OF LAURIETTE
ASHLEY ADAMS PECK**
c. 1840; oil on canvas;
attributed to Erastus Salisbury
Field (1805-1900), New York
City or the Connecticut
River valley. Field was one
of America's most prolific folk
painters, producing over a
thousand paintings. *Courtesy
Museum of American Folk Art.*

Like the European portraitists they mimicked, the American limners were overwhelmingly
male and generally worked in oils. There were, however, a few women such as Ruth Henshaw
Bascom (1772-1848) and quite a few, men and women, who worked in watercolors, pastels, or
other mediums. One of the most interesting watercolorists was Lewis Miller (1796-1882) of York,
Pennsylvania who devoted much of his long life to meticulously chronicling the faces, figures, and
scenes of his native community.

By the mid-19th century most professional painters of folk portraits had turned to other trades
(including photography). However, amateurs continued in the field throughout the Victorian era,
and in the present century the rebirth of folk painting has spawned a new generation, including
such important figures as John Kane (1870-1934) and Larry Zingale, who continues to contribute
to this fine tradition.

**GEORGE WASHINGTON
ON HORSEBACK** c. 1830-1850;
watercolor, ink, and pencil
on paper; Pennsylvania.
This historical painting in the
fraktur manner presents one
of the most popular subjects
of patriotic folk art. *Courtesy
Museum of American Folk Art.*

PORTRAIT OF A WOMAN
c. 1820; oil on canvas,
by John Brewster, Jr. (1766-1854),
Maine. Brewster, a deaf mute,
was a widely traveled artist working
throughout New England for almost
half a century. *Courtesy Sotheby's.*

PORTRAIT OF MARY KINGM
c. 1845; oil on canvas; by Susan C. Wate
(1823-1900), New York or New Jers
Waters was one of the very few recogniz
female portrait artists of the 19th century, a
her work is in great demand. *Courtesy Sotheb*

PORTRAIT OF WOMAN WITH WATERING CAN
c. 1830; watercolor on paper; attributed to Elizabeth Glazer,
Baltimore, Maryland. Glazer, a prolific artist, is known
also for her poetry and needlework. *Courtesy Sotheby's.*

ORTRAIT OF BOY WITH PARROT
1815; watercolor and ink on paper;
tributed to Jacob Maentel (c.1763-1863),
nnsylvania. Maentel, one of the most im-
rtant American folk watercolorists, produced
zens of small portraits. *Courtesy Sotheby's.*

PORTRAIT OF BOY WITH RABBITS
1831; oil on canvas; by John Bradley (d. 1874);
New York or Connecticut. Bradley, like many
American folk painters, embellished his work
with images taken from European prints,
such as the castle seen here. *Courtesy Sotheby's.*

ORTRAIT OF THE TOW SISTERS
1854; watercolor on paper; by Mary
n Smith. Like much early folk painting,
is is a rendition of a period lithograph,
he Two Sisters," by an artist more adept
painting than spelling. *Courtesy Sotheby's.*

Silhouettes

For those who could not afford even Matthew Prior's bargain- basement price of $2.92 for a "flat picture," there was always the silhouette cutter. The origin of the term tells much about the medium: the word is supposed to have been taken from the name of an 18th-century French minister of finance, Etienne de Silhouette, notorious for his frugality. Requiring only paper and scissors to create and selling for as little as twenty-five cents, the silhouette was indeed the thrifty alternative to a portrait.

There are three basic silhouette types: the hollow-cut, which consists of a profile cut from white paper and placed over a piece of darker paper or fabric; the cut-and-paste type in which a silhouette cut from darker material is glued to a lighter ground; and the painted silhouette which is not cut. All three types might be embellished with details in pencil, watercolor, or bronze powder.

While some silhouette artists cut their work freehand, most employed one of several patented mechanical devices called Pantographs which allowed adjustment of image size. Dexterity increased rapidity of production; one silhouettist, William King (1754-) of Salem, Massachusetts claimed to have cut twenty thousand profiles or "shades" at a rate of one every six minutes. King's advertisement in the *Salem Gazette* for July 27, 1804, stated that

> he flatters himself, from the exactness of his profiles and the moderateness of the price
> (only twenty-five cents for two likenesses of one person) he shall give a pleasing satis-
> faction to those who favor him with a call.

Although some portrait painters also cut silhouettes, most were done by specialists. Like limners, they often were itinerants; however, there was frequently an element of theatre involved as well. Some silhouette cutters such as Charles Wilson Peale of Philadelphia (1741-1826) had their own studios or "museums" in which their work was displayed. Others turned handicaps to their advantage. Miss M.A. Honeywell (active 1806-1848), having been born without hands or feet, cut with scissors gripped between her teeth and signed her work, "Cut without hands by M.A. Honeywell." Another, the armless Master Sanders K.G. Nellis, is pictured in the *Salem Advertiser* for January 29, 1836 cutting silhouettes with his toes. He also played the cello and shot a bow and arrow with the same extremities. One suspects that the popularity of such artists was achieved more through spectacle than through skill.

Even more so than the portrait painter, the silhouette cutter was affected by the coming of the camera, which could provide a more accurate and eventually less expensive image. By 1850 nearly all had ceased to pursue this career.

HOLLOW-CUT SILHOUETTES, HUSBAND AND WIFE c. 1820-1840; cut paper with ink; New England. The subjects' collars have been finely dilineated with ink. *Private Collection.*

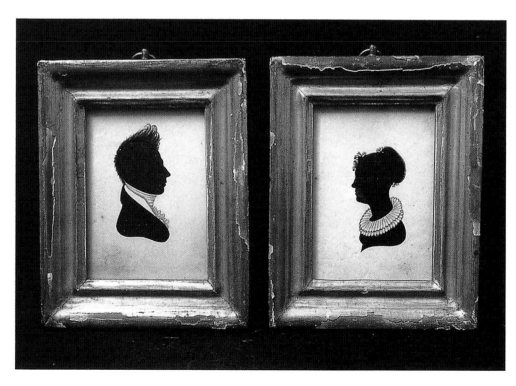

HOLLOW-CUT SILHOUETTE OF A MAN c. 1820-1840; cut paper embellished with ink on fabric; New York. The outer contour of the cut-out paper creates the image and is backed with dark fabric. Like most silhouettes, this one is unsigned. *Private Collection.*

Genre Painting

Genre paintings, scenes of everyday life in home and community, have a long history. Sixteen[th] century Flemish artists like Pieter Brueghel the Elder (1525-1569) created genre paintings wh[ich] hang in every major museum. Similar if less well-known paintings have long been done [by] American folk artists. These range from simple interior scenes through views of individual far[ms] or factories to larger scale compositions such as those of Joseph H. Hidley (1830-1872), w[ho] devoted much of his life to picturing his native Poestenkill, New York.

Many 19th-century American genre paintings were done by professional artists such as Fritz Voght (active 1850-1900) whose work was used to illustrate numerous business directories a[nd] atlases, so popular during the period. However, there were many who worked for the sheer pl[ea]sure of it, including one of our best-known folk artists, Edward Hicks (1780-1849)[, a] Pennsylvanian whose remarkable farm scenes and "Peaceable Kingdoms" are valued in the hu[n]dreds of thousands of dollars.

In the present century genre painting has been graced by the presence of the internationa[lly] acclaimed Grandma Moses (Anna Mary Robertson, 1860-1961) whose renderings of bucc[olic] scenes were instrumental in the establishment of the "memory painting" school of artists wh[ose] work reflects their memory of childhood life in what many seem to have regarded as happ[ier] times. Grandma Moses articulated this artistic philosophy best when she remarked that "thi[ngs] now go faster, in olden times things were not so rushed. I think people were more content, m[ore] satisfied with life than they are today."

Genre painters often relied heavily on period prints for inspiration. Grandma Moses ackno[wl]edged her debt to Currier and Ives lithographs, and a more recent artist who works in the sa[me] vein, Mattie Lou O'Kelley of Atlanta, Georgia (1908-) has sometimes taken her cue from ill[us]trations in *The Saturday Evening Post* and similar popular magazines. In all cases, however, [the] print is but a starting point for the artist, who reworks the theme to produce a unique and p[er]sonal expression.

An important aspect of the genre field is history painting, or the capturing on canvas or ot[her] mediums of important national and world events. Here again there is a long history, dating ba[ck] to the Greeks a[nd] Romans who describ[ed] their martial triump[hs] in clay or on fresco[ed] walls. As early as t[he] 18th century, t[he] American painter Jo[hn] Durand pointed out [to] readers of his adverti[se]

Eliza with Poor Puss.
Published by B. Bramell, No. 572, North Second Street, Philadelphia.

Sacred to the Memory

John Noyes Little,

born Sepr 10th 1798, died Jany 25th 1810.

nts in *The New-York Gazette or the ekly Post-Boy* (April 11, 1768) that

History-painting, besides being extremely ornamental, has many important uses. It presents to our View, some of the most interesting Scenes recorded in ancient or modern History.

.merican folk painters have recreated rything from major battles of the rolution, War of 1812, and Civil War biblical and mythological events. .ong the greatest of these artists was .stus Salisbury Field (1805-1900), ose gigantic painting, *Historical .nument of The American Republic*, (c. '6) is thirteen feet long and incorpo- es numerous vignettes from the public's history, along with miniature traits of the founding fathers and a arre architectural scheme.

emorial Paintings

Memorial paintings, produced for a atively brief period in the early 19th tury, were largely a reflection of ial mores. Women, while denied

MEMORIAL PICTURE
c.1820-1840; needlework
and watercolor; New England.
Such a sentimental and
romantic scene as a tomb
with a weeping willow
surrounded by mourners
in solemn garb makes this a
traditional memorial. *Courtesy
Museum of American Folk Art.*

ess to the trades and professions, were expected not only to supervise the home but also to be : chief mourners of the all-too-common departed. In furtherance of this objective, girls attend- ; boarding or finishing schools were taught to create mourning pictures, watercolor or mixed- dia (watercolor and needlework) paintings which typically featured a tomb, weeping willow es, and one or more despondent (usually female) figures, often dressed in classical garb quite suited to the period.

The earliest mourning pictures were based on English prints depicting Washington's tomb (fol- ving his death in 1799) and were usually of needlework. By the early 1800s these had been gely replaced by watercolor versions which, while still including the motifs described above, ded such embellishments as painted backgrounds (which might include a village or a college), gels, birds, and a variety of flowers and trees. The mourners, rather that being clad in classical wns as in earlier pictures, were frequently clad in period dress. Evolving attitudes toward death d changes in the roles of women gradually brought an end to mourning pictures; few were pro- ced after 1840.

Since most women made only one or two mourning pictures, these artists are, for the most part, t as well known as those who worked in other fields. One name, however, that of the accom- shed Eunice Pinney (1770-1849) of Connecticut, has survived, probably because she left behind variety of historical watercolors and genre scenes as well as memorials.

EMORIAL PICTURE c. 1820-1830; needlework and watercolor; :w England. The earlier memorials were done primarily in :dlework with watercolor backgrounds. *Private Collection.*

Gravestone Art

Much can be learned of a society from way it treats its dead, and American reverence for the departed is reflected in the fi ly carved stones used to mark their pass While the earliest or poorest settlers ha be content with a rude field stone or a wo en cross, by the mid-1600s decorated me rials began to appear in New England's b ial grounds.

The earliest carvers were untrained r from allied crafts such as leatherwork cabinetry, or stonecutting, who found demand and met it. By the mid-18th cer ry, though, a class of gravestone art emerged. What they produced reflec what was regarded as suitable in the com nity. Under the stern gaze of the Puritans whom death was regarded as a deserved e stones were adorned with a death's hea pair of crossed bones, or a figure of the g reaper himself.

Benevolence prevailed in the 1700s the skull became a winged cherub "soul," often accompanied by a rich f ral background, as in the work Zerubbabel Collins (1733-1797) Lebanon, Connecticut and Benningt Vermont.

By 1800 classical motifs such as the fun al urn, tomb, and weeping willow appear making apparent a certain similarity betw gravestone carving and memorial art of same period. Indeed, one suspects that same prints which inspired the school artist may well have influenced the ru stonecutter.

During the 1840s, however, class motifs gradually gave way to the romantic and eclectic designs of the Victorian era. Religi symbols, the hand pointing upward to heaven, and the open bible were popular among ad believers, and such varied motifs as the mortar and pestle, quill pen, anchor, gun, or flag in cated the craft or military service of the deceased. Doves and lambs frequently adorned tombs of children.

While only a few carvers signed their work, most were amazingly consistent in style. As a res it has been possible for researchers to identify a substantial number of artists through second evidence such as estate inventories, bills, and church documents.

TOMB- OR GRAVESTONE
1862; carved marble.
Few funereal symbols are
more portentous than the
finger pointing heavenward.
Graveyard, Fortsville, New York.

TOMB- OR GRAVESTONE 1796; carved marble; by Zerubbabel Collins (1733-1797), Bennington, Vermont.
Dozens of Collins's stones can be found in Vermont and eastern New York, yet no two are quite alike.
Graveyard, Argyle, New York.

CHAPTER 2

FOLK ART AROUND THE HOUSE

There was a time when historians and antiquarians viewed our ancestors as a group of solemn Puritans who lived in houses with whitewashed walls and rejected all interior decoration. Recent studies, however, have shown that, in general, the first Americans loved color, painting their walls red, yellow, and blue and filling their homes with carved and decorated furniture and accessories. That this was the case is hardly surprising, since these settlers came from European nations where such decorative embellishment was customary.

On the other hand, religious strictures sometimes led to criticism of those who wanted a bit of color. In her *Home Life In Colonial Days*, Alice Morse Earle notes that a Salem, Massachusetts resident named Archer was thus mocked by a Puritan neighbor for painting a room: "Well! Archer has set us a fine example of expense—he has laid one of his rooms in oil."

One suspects that less objection was made to carved and painted utensils, as these not only were commonly made at home, but were also often gifts expressing affection for loved ones. Even the stern Cotton Mather would allow for that!

What is often surprising is the high artistic quality of the work involved. Most early settlers were, by necessity, jacks-of-all-trades familiar with saw and hammer, paintbrush and anvil. As a result they were often able to create remarkably fine pieces of folk art. And, of course, it was the best that was treasured and has come down to us. Few mediocre pieces have survived the centuries.

CHILD'S SLED c. 1870-1900; saw-cut pine with free-hand and stencil-painted decoration, northeastern United States. Patriotic motifs such as the eagle and the flag were common on 19th-century childrens' toys. *Courtesy Joel and Betty Schatzberg.*

ROOSTER c. 1865-1875; carved and painted pine with gesso; by William Schimmel; Carlisle, Pennsylvania. An itinerant carver, Schimmel often traded his work for room and board. Today it is highly valued. *Courtesy Museum of American Folk Art.*

Household Carving

Handmade and -shaped utensils were common in early American houses a continued to be made, either through whim or necessity, until the end of the 1 century. Spoons, dippers, and spatulas of pine, maple, or cherry were carved fanciful shapes, such as a spoon with a human or animal head (a custom dating the Middle Ages). Lathe-turned wooden bowls were often painted in bright c ors, as were a variety of covered containers used for storage. In some cases th were made by a local craftsman, but often they were produced in the home a gift. So valued were the storage containers that their owner's name of appeared on the piece, as with a small, round pantry box which is decorated w a heart and inscribed, "MERCY NEEDHAM'S BOX/Sep. 13, 1815."

Simple household tools were also often made at home: rolling pins (the earli had no handles, later examples one and finally two), mortars and pestles, spatu and the lollipop- shaped butter paddles used in the dairy. Some were painted in hues, others, especially in Pennsylvania, might have incised names and desig Much of this work was done with a knife or chisel, though sometimes a simple w lathe motivated by a springy tree was employed to turn basic forms.

Greater skill was required to shape bu prints and molds which were used to impr designs upon fresh butter. The craftsm would carve a decorative figure such as a c (most appropriate), swan, eagle, ear of corn, bundle of wheat on the flat surface of a ha dled, round wooden "print" with which blo of butter were stamped. Molds into which b ter was pressed were similarly carved. Th were even rolling pins covered with figu about their circumference so that they mi be rolled across a sheet of butter. All were ha shaped in the most charming manner.

Closely related were Springerle boa and gingerbread prints, oblong blocks cherry or walnut into which were whitt up to a dozen shallow relief carvings of p ple, birds, animals, flowers, and fru Cookie dough pressed over such a m would retain the designs. Much larger w the cherry or mahogany New Year's c boards made for bakery use. Oval in sh and as much as twenty-five inches lo these were adorned with complex compo tions, sometimes featuring Geo Washington on horseback, the Americ eagle, or other patriotic motifs. Best kno among the carvers of these is John Con of New York City (active 1827-1835).

ARMCHAIR c. 1780-1800; turned, carved, and painted hardwood; Framington-Avon-Sims area of Connecticut. The elaborate carving of hearts on this chair is one of the more whim decorations found in American furniture. *Ex. Lillian Blankley Cogan Collection.*

TRAMP-ART PEDESTAL BOX
c. 1900-1920; carved and notched pine with interior lined in satin, northeastern United States. Decorative boxes like this were often used to store jewelry or keepsakes. *Courtesy Kelter-Malcé Antiques.*

WATER COOLER c. 1830-1850; salt-glazed stoneware with incised, blue-filled eagle decoration; Jacob Van Wickle and James Morgan, Old Bridge, New Jersey. Ornate pieces such as this were usually made on special order or as gifts from the potter. *Private Collection.*

PICTURE FRAME c.1860-1890; carved and painted pine; northeastern United States.
The tinted tintype of a beloved family member is set within a one-of-a-kind folk frame. *Private Collection.*

PICTURE FRAME, BACK VIEW The reverse of the picture frame shown (at left) bears inlaid, punch-decorated, and polychrome painted hearts—symbols of love and affection. *Private Collection.*

Painted Furniture and Accessories

Though all early settlers decorated their household furnishings, none did it with mor verve than the Germanic settlers of Pennsylvania. From the 17th until the end of the 19t century they produced an unending stream of richly painted chests, cupboards, bureau and tables.

Perhaps best known of these are the dower chests in which young women stored quilts an linens to be used after marriage. Given as gifts by parents or swain, these were often date and bore the name of the woman or couple and that of the manufacturer. Made of pine o poplar and decorated on the front and top with polychrome baskets of tulips, unicorns, pir wheels, stars, and other traditional motifs, these storage pieces were once found in near! every Pennsylvania Dutch home. Today, the best examples by makers such as Christia Seltzer (1749-1831) of Jonestown, Pennsylvania, will be found only in museums.

Even as late as the 1870s cabinetmakers in the state's Mahantango Valley were turnin out chests of drawers adorned with brightly colored birds and flowers. Even more pop ular, both in Pennsylvania and in New England, were small storage boxes for sewin materials, handkerchiefs, or other "sundries." These were often the products of youn women attending academies, who would decorate boxes (obtained from cabinetmaker: with complex landscapes and classical scenes. This "academy painting" was also applie to the tops of small tables.

Other useful household items such as pipe and salt boxes, looking glass and picture frame and clock faces were also painted and decorated. Initially this was freehand work in oils, b by the 1820s the availability of stencils and metallic bronze and silver powders resulted in movement toward more mechanical and less individual designs.

While much painted decoration was pictorial, there was even more that was abstrac Furniture makers regularly covered everything from chairs to beds with a coat of red, blu or green paint, often designed to disguise the fact that the piece was made from sever woods of different colors and grains. More sophisticated decorators even enhanced the work with graining and marbleizing: the application, using sponges, brushes, and met

DOWER CHEST c. 1790-1810; polychrome painted pine; Pennsylvania. Designed for storage of a young woman's dowry, these chests were elaborately decorated with flora and fauna. *Courtesy Marna Anderson Gallery.*

STORAGE POT c. 1860-1870; salt-glazed stoneware with free-hand decoration in cobalt blue; New York or Pennsylvania. The word "Union" suggests that the piece dates to the Civil War era. *Courtesy Joel and Betty Schatzberg.*

GAMEBOARD c. 1900-1920; painted pine; New York. Created for Chinese checkers, a game played with marbles within the area of a six-pointed star, this piece exerts a strong appeal through its bold design and vivid coloration. *Private Collection.*

ombs, of a surface that imitated woodgrain or marble. Thus, a skilled workman might transform a plain pine ressing table into one that appeared to be of mahogany ith a marble top.

Not content with these faux finishes, others plied their ools and colors to create fanciful swirling compositions in right reds, blues, yellows, and greens that bore no resemlance to anything found in nature, but evoked a most favorle response from their color-conscious customers. In New rsey and the Hudson Valley area of New York other cabietmakers produced massive storage pieces called kasten, hich were decorated in shades of gray (*grisaille*) with patrns featuring classical urns, fruit, and flowers.

The extensive repertoire of these craftsmen is reflected in 1805 advertisement placed by the Baltimore chair makers, hn and Hugh Finlay (active c. 1803-1833):

CANE SEAT CHAIRS, SOFAS, RECESS and WINDOW SEATS of every description and all colors, gilt ornamented and varnished in a stile not equalled on the continent—with real Views, Fancy Landscapes, Flowers, Trophies of Music, War, Husbandry, Love, &,&.

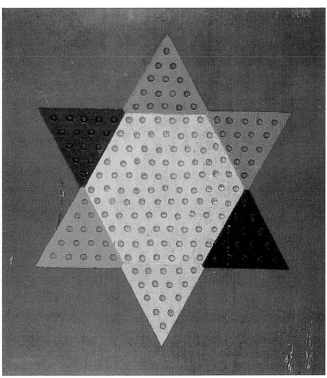

oday the most frequently encountered decorated chairs are
se that were made and marked (c. 1818-1843) by the
nnecticut turner, Lambert Hitchcock (1795-1852).
chcock, who painted his products with a combination of sten-
and freehand work, gave his name to a whole category of
ss-produced furnishings, many of which were still being made
he last decades of the century.

CLOCK FACE
c. 1800-1820;
olychrome painted
ine; New England.
Many early clock
faces became, in
effect, minature
folk paintings.
Author's Collection.

IRLIGIG
930-1940;
ted wood;
nnecticut.
irligigs of
shape, a witch
se arms spin
ne wind, were
le from plans
ted in *Popular*
banics magazine.
ate Collection.

TWO CHESTS
c. 1835-1870; smaller example: grain-painted; the larger: sponged in gray on a putty ground; New England. Neither of these fanciful finishes is intended to resemble a natural wood surface. *Courtesy Marna Anderson Gallery.*

CHECKERBOARD
c. 1900-1925; painted hardwood board with iron feet; Connecticut. A large number of home-made checkers and parcheesi boards exist, made mostly by people unwilling to pay for a factory-produced example. *Courtesy Kelter-Malcé Antiques.*

INKWELL AND SAN
1773; salt-glazed stonew with incised, blue-fi decoration; by Will Crolius, New York, New Y This object, in the shape heart, is a rare and attrac desk piece. *Private Collect*

Figural Art in Metal

An impressive variety of folk art forms appear in wrought and cast iron. In some cases, as with doorstops (door porters to the English), the object is a folk form unto itself; one need think only of the numerous doorstops—ships, baskets of flowers, human figures, birds, and animals—produced by American foundries between 1880 and 1940. Typically, these were cast then painted in bright colors. Since they were made to suit popular taste, designs included some highly topical items: baseball players, Mickey Mouse, a young woman dressed as a flapper, nursery rhyme characters like Little Red Riding Hood, and even Uncle Sam. The great popularity of these doorstops has led to numerous reproductions, and collectors must be wary.

Another category, stoves, includes everything from simple six-plate woodburners embossed with representations of sailing ships, Victorian women, or various floral patterns, to large cast iron coal stoves made in the shape of towers or houses, sometimes crowned with representations of George and Martha Washington. Among other popular and readily available examples of folk art in metal are the andirons employed in fireplaces, both early- American and present-day. Andirons come in various shapes: Hessian soldiers, George Washington, blackamoors, sailors, ducks, geese, dogs, cats with glowing green glass eyes, and even leaping trout. Most date c. 1850-1930 and were originally painted, but they have usually lost their color to the flames. The earliest examples have the dogs soldered to the figures or a dovetail attachment. Nuts and bolts join the dogs in most 19th-century andirons.

Hitching posts of cast iron with rings to which a horse's reins might be secured were a standard fixture before most Victorian homes, shops, and public buildings, and they were usually crowned with a finial. As one might suspect, this was customarily a horse head. However, other forms are known, including human and eagle heads, clenched fists, geometric shapes such as spheres or octagons, and baskets of flowers. There were also a few hitching posts in fully developed human form, most notably the jockey and the young slave, the latter an extremely fine form, sensitively sculpted.

Mill weights were used to counterbalance the blades of the great windmills which pumped well water to nourish midwestern crops. Weighing from fifteen to fifty pounds, they come in a variety of purely decorative forms: squirrels, ducks, chickens, cats, and birds, as well as moons, stars and abstract shapes. Largely unknown to Eastern collectors until the 1970s, these pieces have, despite their weight and general awkwardness, attracted a faithful following. As with decorative stoves, though, few people have space for a large collection.

Far easier to handle and display are the small cast iron match safes which once hung in every kitchen. Hundreds of different types are known; so many, in fact, that collectors may specialize in a single area such as patriotic, floral, or advertis-

BOOT SCRAPER
c. 1990-1930; sheet iron;
midwestern United States.
No longer in use, these
quaint pieces are now
displayed as folk sculpture.
Private Collection.

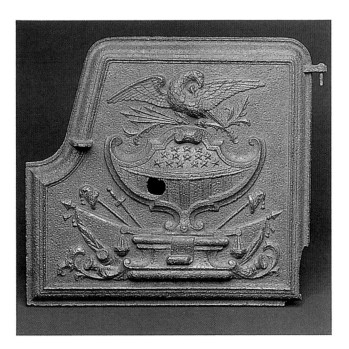

STOVE DOOR c. 1830-1850;
cast iron with embossed
eagle and trophies of war;
Troy, New York. Heating
and cooking stoves, once
the focal point of a room,
were often lavishly decorated.
Ex. Author's Collection.

ANDIRONS c. 1900-1920;
polychrome painted cast iron,
New York or New England.
Hessian soldiers are among
the most common subjects
for figural andirons. Others
in the same patriotic vein are
eagles, Columbia, and George
Washington. *Private Collection.*

(many were promotional give-aways). These are often found in original paint, and most desir-
_e_ are the rarities: black Americana, political campaign themes, and one-of-a-kind pieces.

The bootjack was another popular device, used to remove boots and shoes. Best known, of
urse, is the slightly scatological "Naughty Nellie," but other examples include an oversized bee-
and a longhorn steer whose horns serve to pry off the recalcitrant footwear.

A variety of iron benches, chairs, and tables used on patios and lawns were also quite common.
stic examples, with backs, seats, and arms in the shape of leafy branches, are much sought after
_ay,_ as are a variety of garden urns (some four feet high), flower pots, and even cast iron fish
_ks._ All were embossed with decorative floral patterns and are greatly favored by contemporary
dscape designers and decorators.

olky metal door knockers shaped like hands, eagles, or flags greeted the visitor to the American
_me_ of the past. Within the kitchen were found a multitude of cast iron objects, including fig-
_l_ trivets upon which hot plates might rest, and the stands used for holding flatirons. These lat-
, like match safes, were frequently business give-aways, incorporating the name or logo of a
indry or a company which manufactured kitchen utensils.

ess common are painted cast iron picture and mirror frames. World War I spurred the man-
cture of iron picture frames decorated with cannons and American flags, presumably designed
house an image of a son or husband fighting in Europe. Earlier Victorian frames are in the Art
ouveau manner.

Following Page:
ANDIRONS c. 1870-1900;
New England or southern
United States. These
African forms represent
one of several variations
which include figures clad
as sailors. *Private Collection.*

CIGAR HOLDER
c. 1900-1925; carved
and painted wood,
incised "Habanas";
eastern United States.
This wall-hung
receptacle was used
for cigars or matches.
Ex Jay Johnson Collection.

OT JACK
_880-1920; painted
_t iron, New York.
_is object, in the shape
_a beetle, was designed
_ease the effort of
_noving one's boots.
_e boot heel is placed
_ween the beetle's
_ngated feelers, which
_d the boot in place
_ile the foot is with-
_wn. *Private Collection.*

39

EAGLE c. 1870-1890;
carved and painted pine with
gesso; by William Schimmel
(1817-1890); Carlisle,
Pennsylvania. Eagles, with
wing spreads up to three feet,
were Schimmel's favorite birds.
Private Collection.

WINDMILL WEIGHT c. 1880-1910;
painted cast iron; attributed to
Elgin Windmill Power Company,
Elgin, Illinois. These heavy pieces
were originally mounted high on
the windmill to balance the propeller
weight. Now, with their prime purpose
gone, collectors may examine them
at close range for their aesthetic value.
Courtesy American Primitive Gallery.

DOORSTOP c. 1930-194
painted cast iron; Oh
Cartoon figures and storybo
characters, such as Lit
Red Riding Hood sho
here, were popular doorst
subjecs. *Private Collecti*

Religious Painting and Carving

In most areas of the United States religious painting and sculpture is not found in the home or, at present, is largely confined to commercial reproductions. A notable exception is the Southwest, where in states such as New Mexico and Arizona Spanish-Americans have long cherished religious folk art. Local craftsmen known as *santeros* produced three types of art: large, polychromed carved altar screens (*reredos*), paintings on pine or cottonwood panels called *retablos*, and figural carvings, *bultos*. The subjects were saints and the holy family and the inspiration was provided by religious prints or the few classical paintings brought in long ago from Mexico.

With the exception of altar screens which were intended for the adobe churches, these pieces were produced mainly for the small shrines or *nichos* found in every believer's home. Consequently, most were quite small. *Bultos* were generally two feet or less in height, and the typ-

ADAM AND EVE 1965; carved pine; George T. Lopez, Cordoba, New Mexico. Lopez is a member of a family that for generations has carved *bultos*, or Spanish-American religious figures. Unlike most *santeros*, he often does not paint his figures. *Collection Rubens Teles.*

REREDO OR ALTAR SCREEN c. 1840-1890; carved and painted wood; from the chapel of Our Lady of Talpa, Talpa, New Mexico. *Courtesy Taylor Museum, Colorado Springs Fine Arts Center.*

ical *retablo* measured about eight by twelve inches. An exception was the *bulto a vestir*, a cloth-covered fra[me]work with carved head and hands. Often four feet tall, these were primarily church furnishings.

Though long unappreciated outside the Southwest, *bultos* and *retablos* have come to be recognized as am[ong] the most powerful and moving of American folk art forms. Artists like Jose Rafael Aragon (active c. 18[00-] 1835) and Fray Andres Garcia (active c. 1748-1778) are now highly regarded.

By the late 1800s the *santeros* had begun to vanish, their work replaced by inexpensive religious prints s[old] at trading posts. However, in the last few decades a new group of artists has emerged to carry on the age-[old] tradition. Ironically, though, the work of such 20th-century carvers as Jose Dolores Lopez (1868-1938[) of] Cordoba, New Mexico is sold mostly to collectors rather than believers. Some of these sculptors, such [as] Felipe Archuleta (1910-) of Tesuque, New Mexico have expanded their repertoire to include non-religi[ous] carvings. His lively animal carvings have been exhibited at several major museums.

Religious carvings and paintings have been made during this century in other areas of the country as w[ell.] One of the best known 20th-century folk carvers was John Perates (1895-1970) of Portland, Maine. Pera[tes]

SAINT LUKE
c. 1935-1945;
carved and
painted oak
bas relief; by
John Perates
(1894-1970);
Portland, Maine.
Perates, a skilled
cabinetmaker,
produced a series
of reliefs and
an altar for his
Greek Orthodox
church. *Private
Collection.*

created a monumental grouping [of] painted relief carvings based on [the] life of Christ. These were desig[ned] for installation in his church, [but] most pieces have found their [way] into public and private collectio[ns.] Perates' work reflects another [old] country tradition, that of the pai[nt]ed icon.

On a much smaller scale are [the] biblical carvings of Edgar Tols[on] (1904-) of Compton, Kentuc[ky.] Born in the Appalachians and h[eir] to a long tradition of whittli[ng,] Tolson created with knife and chi[sel] a variety of delicate, sparsely-c[ol]ored pieces based on such themes [as] the expulsion from paradise and [the] story of Cain and Abel. His sto[ny] faced figures have the power a[nd] frontality of Gothic images.

THE NAZARENE CHRI[ST
c. 1850-1860; carved and pain[ted] cottonwood with cotton r[obe] and horsehair wig; north[ern] New Mexico. A figure of this ty[pe,] known as a *bulto a vestir*, wo[uld] most likely be intended a[s a] devotional object in a small par[ish] church. *Courtesy Taylor Muse[um,] Colorado Springs Fine Arts Cen[ter.]*

Do Flag save the old Flag the White Red and Blue
Shall wave o'er a nation unbroken and true
Rise up and defend it, ye sons of the Brave.

CHAPTER 3

PASSING TIME: FOLK ART AS HOBBY

s the 19th century advanced, leisure time became a greater part of American life; labor-saving devices in the home, on the farm, and in the factory allowed more people to have more e time. In the period before movies, radio, and television, this time was often occupied by what e might term creative hobbies, activities that were both interesting and often productive of nething useful and attractive. This was especially true in the case of middle- and upper-class men, who were the beneficiaries of both new domestic appliances and an influx of cheap, immint domestic labor. To fill her newly acquired spare time the lady of the house often turned to times such as theorem painting and calligraphy.

uch leisure-time undertakings were not confined to women. Games and art activities like sandber painting were regarded as acceptable for mixed groups, and many men excelled in calliphic drawing. None of this would have been regarded as useful by the Puritans, but in the 19th itury the belief that "idle hands do the devil's work" was reinterpreted to allow those hands asurable as well as proctive activities.

Crafts indulged in pririly by men, such as cane l whimsey carving and e making of tramp art jects, reflected a general niliarity with the jackife at a time when most les had a certain amount mechanical facility, and ts were more often handde than store-bought.

EMBROIDERY ON PAPER 1848; multi-colored silk thread embroidery on rag paper; by Eda Brown, northeastern United States. The artist has brought freshness and simplicity to a common 19th-century theme. Textile folk art of this sort is both rare and desirable. *Courtesy Kelter-Malcé Antiques.*

R COUNTRY IS FREE c. '0; watercolor on paper; by Miller, Illinois. Like many ilar folk paintings, this one s adapted from a 19th-centuCurrier & Ives lithograph. rtesy Merle H. Glick.

THEOREM c. 1830-1850; watercolor on velvet; New England. The classic theorem form was the basket or bowl of fruit, sometimes embellished with a bird or butterfly. *Private Collection.*

Theorem Painting

One of the most popular arts practiced during the 1800s was theorem painting, a form of compo tion in which cardboard stencils of individual elements such as leaves, apples, or gourds were co bined to a whole. These pictures usually took the form of a compote or basket filled to overflow with fruit, flowers, and vegetables, above which hovered a bird or butterfly.

Theorem painting was a most democratic process requiring no formal training. Moreover, by m century newspapers and women's magazines carried advertisements for complete kits with which practice the art. Advice such as the following offered in the publication *Art Recreations* in 1868 is typi

> Theorem Painting...is better shaped to fruits, birds and butterflies, than to landscapes and heads. It will enable you to paint on paper, silk, velvet, crepe, and light colored wool. Lay the theorem on the paper on which you intend to paint....Press the theorem firmly down with weights at each corner and proceed to paint. Commence with a leaf; take plenty of paint, a very little moist, on your brush, and paint in the cut leaf of the theorem....If suc- cessful with a leaf, try a grape.

Despite the various surfaces suggested, most theorem paintings found today were done on velvet, as the watercolors used were less likely to run on this fabric. However, paper and even tin were used. The earliest theorem examples date to the 1850s, and the art was still being practiced the turn of this century.

Calligraphy

Calligraphic art was a byproduct of the ornamental handwriting widely practiced throughout the 19th and early 20th centuries. Often referred to as Spencerian script (for a writing master named Spencer who established a chain of secretarial schools), this highly stylized or "flourished" technique enabled the practitioner not only to write a most readable hand, but also to produce charming pen-and-ink drawings. These delicate works are of great interest today, but they were a minor part of calligraphic training. A typical period text, *Tarble's SELF-INSTRUCTOR IN WRITING AND ITS USES* (1856), devoted only a single example and one paragraph to such illustration, pointedly stating that "no attention should be paid to these, until the other copies are well mastered."

Nevertheless, much of the finest calligraphy extant is in the form of large drawings, typically of birds (eagles were a great favorite), lions, horses, and human figures, done by writing masters as advertisements of their skills. Most are in black and white, though blue and red inks as well as watercolor embellishments were sometimes employed. Few students attained this level of competence, though many learned to produce a nice bluebird as evidenced by the number of such drawings which grace the small autograph books popular among Victorian girls and boys. Removed and mounted, these four-by-seven-inch sketches are often seen in antique shops and shows.

GRISAILLE THEOREM c. 1830-1840; gray wash and pencil on paper; New England. Most theorems were done in bright colors. Examples in shades of gray are rare. *Courtesy Museum of American Folk Art.*

AMERICAN EAGLE, CALLIGRAPHY DRAWINGS 1872; brown ink on paper; by S. Fagley, New York or Pennsylvania. Eagles were a particularly popular subject for calligraphers as well as for artists working in other media during the 19th century. *Courtesy Museum of American Folk Art.*

Sandpaper Paintings

Sandpaper paintings are so named because they were done on a piece of paper covered with adhesive and marble dust, little different from modern sandpaper. These works weren't painted at all, but were executed in charcoal or chalk. The purpose of this odd combination was, through the mingling of black and gray with the gleaming background, to create the mysterious (some would say gloomy) night mood of which Victorians seemed so fond.

While theorems were an individual artistic expression, the sandpaper or graphite painting was often a group exercise. During the late 19th century the drawing contest was a popular after-dinner activity. A painting or print would be placed on an easel, and all assembled would take charcoal and sandpaper in hand. The person who best duplicated the original would be given a small prize for his or her efforts.

Such parlor games were greatly facilitated by the availability in shops and by mail order of kits containing materials and a selection of prints to be copied. It is for this reason that there are many sandpaper works that duplicate the same scene, usually the ruins of an abandoned castle or a classical cityscape. More interesting are one-of-a-kind pieces such as portraits or views of homes or small towns. Some of these also incorporate pastels to enliven the dark palette.

Scissor Cuttings

Though practiced in other parts of the country, paper or scissor cutting is particularly associated with the Pennsylvania Germans, who called the work cherenschnitte and made of it a highly creative folk art. The basic techniques are ones with which every reader is familiar. Figures cut from paper are applied to a background of contrasting color, or a single piece of paper is folded many times and then cut to create a repeating design.

STAG, CALLIGRAPHY DRAWING c. 1830-1870; ink and gray wash on paper; by S.R. Baldwin, northeastern United States. Larger drawings like this one (19 x 15 1/2 inches), were often done by writing masters. Sometimes, needlework design books served as a source for the composition. *Courtesy Museum of American Folk Art.*

VIEW OF THE GENESSE FALLS c. 1829-1860; charcoal on sandpaper, Rochester, New York. The great falls on the Genesee River were the scene of Sam Patch's last leap. Patch, a stunt man, had made several spectacular jumps. He did not survive this one. *Private Collection.*

Among the earliest examples are love [to]kens, the forerunners of the modern [va]lentine. A Connecticut cut-and-pasted [to]ken is based on the traditional design of [a h]eart held or offered in the hand and is [ap]propriately inscribed, "Heart and hand [sh]all never part/When this you see, [re]member me." Pennsylvania pieces (one [as] early as 1754) are more often of the [fol]ded and cut variety, in many cases fur[th]er decorated with watercolors or writ[ten] over with expressions of tenderness. [An] amusing example made in 1875 states, ["T]his thirteenth day of February It was [my] lot to be merry. It was my fortune and [my] lot to draw your name out of the hat," [su]ggesting that the maker had attended a [va]lentine's Eve social gathering with the [re]cipient and had drawn her name in a

MEMORIAL c. 1830-1840; scissor cutting or scherenschnitte; gilt foil on oil cloth; Pennsylvania. Scissor cuttings in gold foil are rare; and even rarer are memorial examples. *Courtesy Museum of American Folk Art.*

HIBISCUS FLOWER, CALLIGRAPHY DRAWING c. 1870-1890; ink and watercolor on paper; New England or Pennsylvania. Americans of the 18th and 19th centuries were intrigued by exotic flowers such as this one. The poem beneath the bloom is by English poet laureate Robert Southey. *Courtesy Museum of American Folk Art.*

lottery, an ancient English custom (and, perhaps, a forerunner of the mod
dating service).

Unusual scherenschnitte variations include examples embellished with hair w
(presumably the maker's hair) and ones in more expensive gold or silver foil. Am
the latter is a rare mourning picture now in the collection of the Museum of Ameri
Folk Art. It features matching tombs, flowers and weeping willow trees.

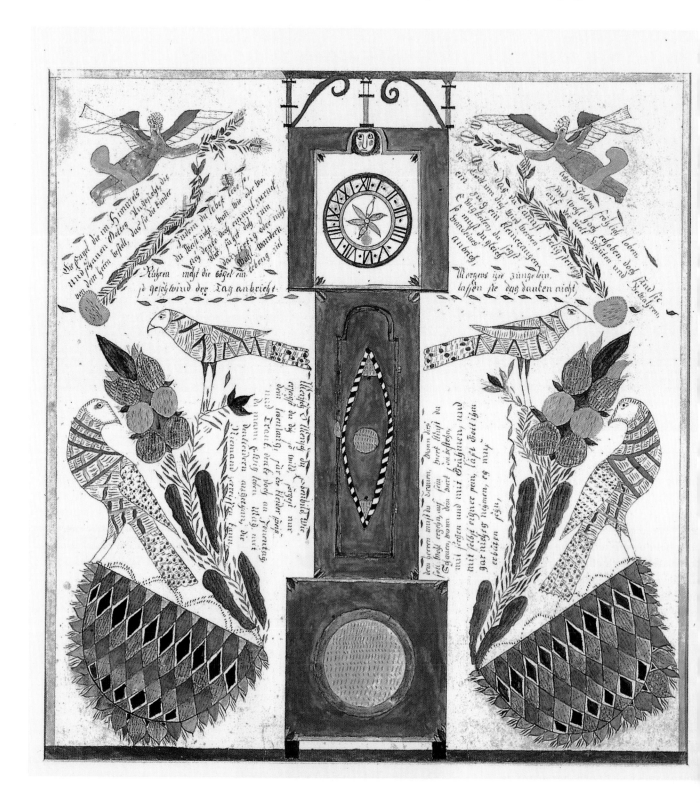

RESIDENCE OF MR. AND MRS. JOHN H. ABEL 1894; crayon and pencil on paper; Fritz G. Voght (active 1850-1900), Stone Arabia, New York. Voght was one of a group of artists who created illustrations for popular 19th-century business directories. *Courtesy Sotheby's.*

THE OLD SCHOOL HOUSE c. 1800-1820; watercolor on paper; New England. This charming piece was probably done by a schoolgirl who attended the pictured female seminary. *Private Collection.*

SPIRITUAL CLOCK FRAKTUR c. 1820-1850; watercolor on paper; Pennsylvania. Thought to reflect religious inspiration, this painting features a clock symbolizing the passage of temporal life. The design is related to that of Pennsyvania birth and marriage frakturs. *Courtesy Sotheby's.*

WASHINGTON   DE KALB   STEUBEN

THE HEROES OF TH

PULASKY   KOSCIUSKO   LA FAYETTE   MUHLENBERG

EVOLUTION

THE HEROES OF THE
REVOLUTION c.
1860-1880; oil on can-
vas; Louis Mader
(c.1842-1892), eastern
United States.
Patriotic paintings like
this, often taken from
period prints, were
popular in the mid-
19th century. *Courtesy
Sotheby's.*

57

Reverse Paintings on Glass

The technique of painting on glass was developed in Asia, spread to the Near East, and beca[me] popular in Italy and France during the 1600s. Introduced into England, it found its way to [the] United States in the early 19th century. Technically, it is a tedious procedure involving first l[ay]ing down the details on the back of a glass sheet and then adding the background—the reverse [of] the normal procedure. Some benefit is derived from the fact that the glass protects the painti[ng,] but this is offset by the fragile nature of the work. Not only is the glass readily broken, but [the] oils also tend to separate from the glass, leading to major restoration problems.

Nevertheless, reverse painting is an extremely popular folk art expression. Among the earli[est] American examples are the glass tablets found in the upper sections of Federal mirrors. Th[ey] often feature a c. 1812 sea battle between British and American warships. Also found, both as in[di]vidual works and as mirror tablets, are portraits of attractive women and theatrical views, as w[ell] as uncommon representations of animals and farmyard scenes.

During the period c. 1880-1920 a large number of reverse glass paintings of American loca[les] were produced. These include three views of the Statue of Liberty with the vessels in the ba[ck]ground changing over time from sailing ships to sail steamers to American warships; several d[ra]matic versions of the Titanic sinking; and numerous other popular examples such as views of [the] White House or resorts like Lake George in the Adirondack Mountains. It is believed that th[ey] were made at small shops in the New York City area, but so far no documentation has emerg[ed.] It is clear, though, that most were based on prints and designed to be sold as tourist items.

Reverse glass painting is still done today. The best-known practitioner is Milton Bond (19[-] 1994) of New York City, whose sparkling depictions of well-known landmarks like the Brook[lyn] Bridge and the Empire State Building are in great demand.

Tinsel painting is a variation of reverse glass painting. Here the design is enhanced by the ad[di]tion to the composition of crinkled foil or bits of mother-of-pearl. Applied to the back of the p[ic]ture, they add a sparkle and glow unique to this form. Though these materials might be added [to] any reverse painting, they are most often found in combination with floral designs, typically a v[ase] or basket of flowers sim[ilar] in composition to the[se] found in theorem paintin[g.] Such pieces are still be[ing] made today.

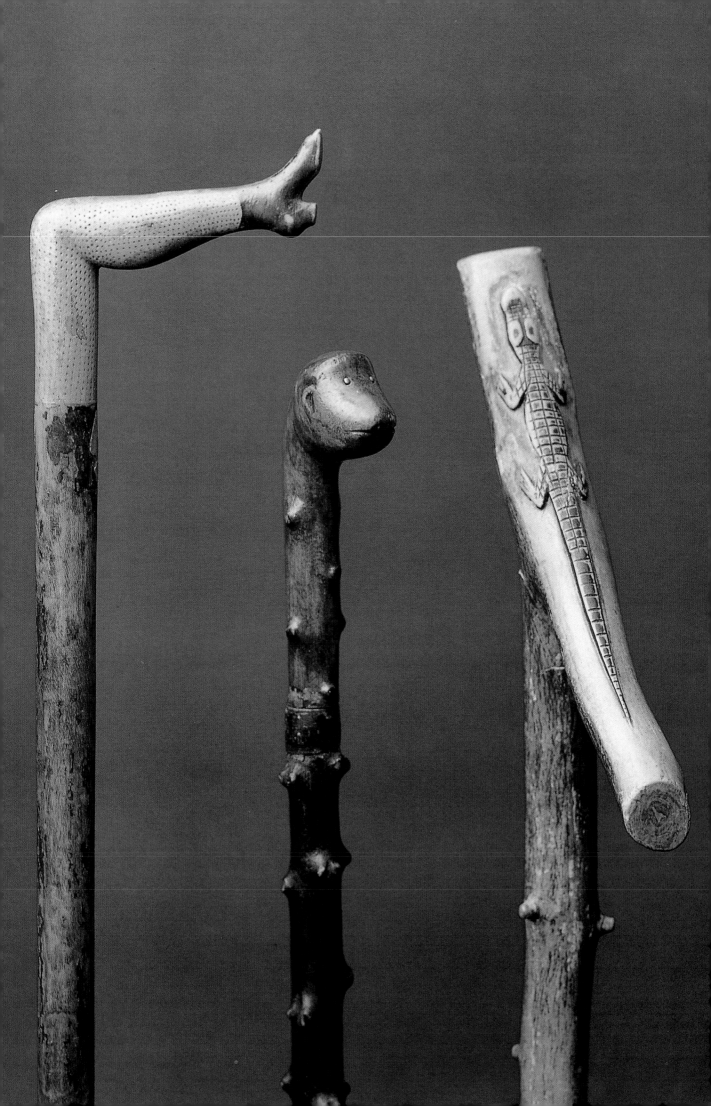

ane and Whimsey Carving

Carving or "whittling" was a common male occupation throughout the past two centuries. ery man and boy carried a jackknife (usually Case or Barlow made) and, except among the high-social echelons, it was long regarded as quite normal to continue whittling while talking, lis-ing to a sermon, or attending a social gathering. The prevalence of this hobby is reflected in e numerous paintings and prints which depict it.

While it was possible to carve any number of different objects, two were particularly popular: es and whimsies. In an age when gout, arthritis, and crippling injuries were common, many n carried canes. These were often intricately worked. In the South, relief-carved snakes, alli-ors, possums, fish, and turtles frequently adorned the walking stick, or, in rare cases, the entire e might be shaped in the form of a single, writhing serpent. Some have suggested that this mplex and bold carving was first developed by black artisans following the African tradition of staff of office, which reflected and enhanced a chief's power and prestige.

Northern walking sticks were more likely to bear incised, often color-filled decorations. Cut into bark, these depicted human figures, animals, birds, and houses. Patriotic motifs like the flag and eagle were also quite popular, particularly in times of national crisis. There was also a continu-on of the European tradition of the mountain or walking staff: a heavy rod into which the climber the names of important mountains he had climbed and the dates of these accomplishments.

Native Americans also made carved canes; among the best-known are an important group pro-ced by an Iroquois craftsman as well as examples from the Northwest coastal tribes. The latter shaped in the form of the totem poles so characteristic of the region, and are related to the ffs of office carried by native shamans or medicine men.

Wash sticks, long fork-like pieces of wood used to stir the wash in wooden tubs (in the days fore modern washing machines) were also often elaborately carved and presented as gifts to men by their husbands. The hearts, flowers, and messages of endearment may have reflected a of guilt at avoiding a difficult and unpleasant task traditionally regarded as "women's work."

Much smaller are the carved whimsies and puzzles made in great quantity by skilled practition-. Some of these, referred to as all-of-a-piece carvings (because they were made from a single ce of wood) are true puzzles: balls within cages or lengths of wooden chain, all carved from a gle block and impossible to separate without breaking. While earlier examples date from the d-19th century, the art has not been lost—puzzle carvings are still being made today. Usually easily-cut pine, they are seldom painted.

The bottle display is another type of whimsey: tiny carved (but rarely painted) elements are serted into a bottle to form a composition. Among these are complete miniature workshops, urch altars, and representations of patriotic scenes. Such work is clearly related to that nautical zzle, the ship in a bottle, but appears to be less common. The only important collection in a ajor institution is that of the Museum of American Folk Art in New York City.

CANE OR WALKING STICK WITH SCULPTURAL HEAD c. 1850-1900; carved hardwood, red stained; New Hampshire. Canes with heavy heads like this were often made by sailors who found them useful weapons in barroom brawls. *Courtesy George Schoelkopf.*

HORSE'S HEAD CANE HEAD OR HANDLE c. 1910-1930; painted pine with glass eyes; New York. Finely carved canes like this are really miniature folk sculptures. *Author's Collection.*

NES OR WALKING STICKS c. 1880-1920; rved and painted hardwood; left to right, orida, New York, and Maine. Though sel-m signed by their makers, canes are distinct rsonal expressions reflecting beliefs, preju-ces, and popular myths. *Author's Collection.*

Tramp Art

Another interesting male pastime, particularly during the early 20th century, was the making objects both large and small from scrap wood, preferably mahogany cigar boxes or fruit crates rough pine. Such things as mirror and picture frames, wall and sewing boxes, pin cushion hol ers, and doll furniture as well as much larger objects like chests of drawers, planters, and even so were made from layers of thin wood nailed or glued together, then decorated with chip or not carving. Many pieces were brightly painted (gold and silver were particularly popular), while ot ers were embellished with bits of glass or colored cloth.

The term "tramp art" reflects a popular belief that these pieces were made by itinerants. N doubt some smaller examples were (many date from the 1930s when the Great Depression forc many men to the road), but larger pieces show marks of a band saw, much too large a tool for hobo to carry about. Moreover, patterns for making tramp art objects appeared frequently in su 20th-century men's how-to magazines as *Popular Mechanics*, and some pieces are known to ha been made in school shop classes.

It should also be noted that such work was not confined to this country; examples made Europe and Canada are known. Whatever its origin, much tramp art has a wonderfully folky qua ity, and it is extremely popular with collectors.

Closely related is "crown of thorns" work, a more delicate technique involving assembling sm pieces of notched wood which are interlocked and overlapped to form an open framework. Th construction lent itself to architectural forms, and many of the relatively few surviving pieces a models of churches or other buildings, though large picture frames are also known. Unlike tran art, crown of thorns pieces were usually left unpainted, weathering to a rich brown surface.

In the Northeast and Canada men, particularly loggers with time on their hands due inclement weather, made another notch-carved form, the spruce gum box. These small contai ers had sliding lids and, unlike tramp art, were made from a single block of wood. They were us ally incised with decorative motifs and bore the recipient's name, and were used to hold spru gum, an early and not especially tasty type of chewing gum.

VIEW OF THE SCHUYLKILL COUNTY ALMSHOUSE 1881; oil on canvas; Charles C. Hofmann (1821-1882), Schuylkill County, Pennsylvania. Hofmann, an indigent alcoholic, often painted the poorhouses in which he took shelter. *Courtesy Sotheby's.*

ABRAHAM LINCOLN c. 1975; carved and painted wooden relief; by Elijah Pierce (1892-1984), Columbus, Ohio. The black artist, Elijah Pierce, favored religious and patri otic images and believed that each of his carvings was a message from God. *Private Collection.*

CHAPTER 4

BLOWING IN THE WIND

′eathervanes

ithout doubt, weathervanes are among the most popular of all American folk art. They also ve by far the longest history of any important folk art object. The weathervane served a dual iction, both as a weather prognosticator and as a symbol of status.

The Romans had metal weathervanes atop their villas, and the 12th-century Viking explorers d warriors utilized similar devices on their longboats. The famous 11th-century Bayeaux pestry depicts a workman mounting a weathervane atop England's Westminster Abbey. During e Middle Ages, the attractive but fragile fabric banners which flew from castles, indicating their ner's rank, were gradually replaced by duplicates made of metal.

Vanes came to America with the earliest colonists, but because of their fragile nature only a few e-1700 examples have survived. These are generally of metal, the most durable construction dium. Sheet iron was probably the initial choice of manufacturers, but by the 18th century pper, which could be formed readily into three-dimensional figures, was preferred. So it mains today, though cast iron, too, has been popular. However, those lacking metal working- lls or the money to pay for a craftsman's products have often produced charming carved and inted wooden vanes.

Traditionally, weathervanes were made in the form of a banneret (mimicking the knights' heraldic mbols) or a cock, but during the past two hundred years many other types have emerged.

annerets

This category includes not only banner-shaped vanes, but also arrows and banner-like forms erced with initials and sometimes dates relating to the owner. An early American example is the

nogram banner placed atop e old Dutch church in rrytown, New York in 1699. ch devices have remained pular for over two centuries; ost are of sheet iron or copper, ough a few wooden examples e known. The arrow pointing own the wind" is, perhaps, the ost naturalistic of weathervane

ROOSTER WEATHERVANE
c. 1790-1820; sheet iron; New Jersey. Like many homemade vanes, this one has a charming folk quality. *Private Collection.*

ODDESS OF LIBERTY EATHERVANE c. 1880-1895; Ilded copper with paint d gilding; attributed to B. & W. T. Westervelt; w York, New York. berty, in various guises, quently appears in weather- ie form. *Private Collection.*

shapes; the large feathered tail pr[]
vides excellent balance and wi[]
surface.

The Cock or Rooster

Almost as old as the banneret[] the weathercock. In the 9th centu[] a Papal decree required that eve[] church should have a vane in t[] form to remind the faithful [] Peter's betrayal of Christ: " I tell y[] Peter, the cock will not crow this d[] until you three times deny m[] (Luke 22:34).

The cock (which might va[] from fighting cock to barnya[] rooster) was very popular in t[] country. One of the remaini[] early examples is the five-foot-t[] gilded weathercock made for [] Boston church in 1721 by t[]

Trotting Horse Weathervane c. 1900-1920; painted corrugated sheet tin; Long Island, New York. The design was taken from a commercially made copper weathervane and may possibly represent Goldsmith Maid, a well-known horse of the day. *Private Collection.*

metal worker Shem Drowne (1683-1744). Roosters, along with eagles and horses, continue be made both here and abroad; artificially aged modern reproductions sometimes find th[] way into antique shops.

Other Birds

The rooster was but one of several birds found in weathervane form. Most often seen today a[] still manufactured are eagles, whose position as the national symbol has long endeared them [] patriotic homeowners as well as to the builders of public facilities like courthouses and town ha[] Almost all are three-dimensional molded copper birds made in factories during the past centu[] Since many were designed to be placed high on large edifices, eagle vanes may be quite lar[] examples with five-foot wingspans are known.

Less often seen is the peaceful dove, though this was the symbol chosen by our nation's f[] commander-in-chief, George Washington. Returning to Mount Vernon in 1783 he ordered t[] type from a Philadelphia craftsman specifying that

> I should like to have a bird...with an olive branch in its mouth. The bird need not be
> large (for I do not expect that it will traverse with the wind and therefore may receive
> the real shape of a bird with spread wings).

Other available avian forms, most rarely seen today, include the swan, ostrich, peacock, phe[] ant, goose, and owl. Most appear not to have been very popular. In some cases price may ha[] been a factor. A three-and-a-half-foot high ostrich was listed in the 1893 catalog of the J.W. Fis[] company at $65, a good deal of money at the time.

Horses

Horses and men have had a long, close association, and it is hardly surprising that the equi[] form is found in a greater variety than any other weathervane. However, there is no evidence th[]

Ram Weathervane c. 1880-1910; molded sheet copper w[] green patina; northeastern United States. Vanes in the shape of fa[] animals were popular with farmers and stockmen. *Private Collecti[]*

ARCHER WEATHERVANE
c. 1900-1920; painted sheet
iron; Massachusetts. Native
Americans were popular subjects for turn-of-the-century
vane makers. *Private Collection.*

the great war horses of the Middle Ages or the fleet steeds of Arabia w
ever the subject of weathervane artists.

In fact, it was not until after the Civil War that American metal sho
began turning out horse weathervanes. Since then dozens of well-kno
variations, almost all of racing rather than work animals, have appea
Many of these, such as the famous trotters, Dexter, Smuggler, and Et
Allen, have been depicted in copper. Most are shown without rider
sulky, perhaps due to the expense of producing the added features.
twenty-two horse vanes illustrated in the A.B. and W.T. Westervelt ca
log issued in 1883, only three featured sulkies and only two, a "fa
horse" and a "horse to wagon," illustrated non-sporting animals.

The beauty of a running or trotting horse is so evident, and so m
wished to have one mounted atop a barn or stable that copies of
commercial vanes (or creations based on contemporary Currier and I
lithographs of famous racers) were made in other materials, such
sheet iron, tin, zinc, and wood. Some of the latter, their original pa
long weathered away, are among the most evocative of American f
sculptures.

Other Animals

A surprisingly large number of other beasts have graced Americ
weathervanes. Some of these we would expect to find. Farmers co
obtain generic bulls, cows, oxen, hogs, goats, and sheep as well as m
specific types (perhaps tailored to their own livestock) such as a sho
horned Jersey cow or the prize-winning Merino ram, Sweepstakes. Su
vanes served as advertisements as well as status symbols.

Domestic animals are less common. There are few cats, and man's b
friend is generally memorialized only as "dog" or "sportsman's do
though a form described as "English hound" is known. The latter is, perhaps, related to the
vanes which head a list of common American wild animal vanes including many variations of de
squirrels, bears, moose, and bison.

It is more difficult to explain the presence on American rooftops of the European boar, the li
and the elephant. It is likely though that the latter two were intended for circuses, traveli
menageries, and zoos.

Fish vanes were produced in quantity for shore dwellers and those who made their living by
sea. Though usually not identified, shape and decoration enable us to recognize such import
food fishes as cod (a replica of which was placed above a Marblehead, Massachusetts church
1748), haddock, and mackerel as well as swordfish, dolphins, and, of course, whales. Less read
explained are vanes in the form of sea serpents and sea horses, dragons, mermaids, and centau

Humans

Commercial manufacturers showed surprisingly little interest in the human form with
exception of the Native American. Indians in many sizes and postures (usually warlike) appear
all the makers' catalogs. One explanation is, perhaps, that several fraternal groups, most nota
the Improved Order of Red Men, took the Indian as a symbol. As a result meeting halls oft
mounted a weathervane in his form.

To these, amateur artists added such interesting vanes as a captain with a spyglass, a whaler w
a horn, farmers with shovels and flails, a hunter, and a swimming man. Most were of polychrom
wood. Commercial makers of metal weathervanes seemed more interested in mythological fi
ures, giving us the drinking god Gambrinus, Diana the Huntress, Mercury, and the angel Gabri

Occupational Vanes

The use of weathervanes as advertisement led to the development of numerous examples whi
indicated the business or profession carried on within a building. Quill pens signified a lawyer

vener; the lyre, a musician; a malt shovel and barrel, a brewery; an
il, a blacksmith; a plow, a farmer; a shoe, either a shoe store or a shoe-
ker; a bicycle-mounted messenger, the telegraph company; a gun, the
al armory; a fireman's trumpet or hook and ladder, the firehouse; a saw,
rpenter; and a tobacco leaf or cigar, a tobacconist.

o popular were such devices that a large company which installed
tning rods made it a practice to give small weathervanes to its rural
tomers: pigs, cows, or chickens, depending on what they raised on
farm.

ansportation

is especially appropriate that a vane constantly in motion should
ict a form of transportation, and a variety of these are known. Earliest,
doubt, are ship weathervanes, most of which were made of metal or a
nbination of wooden hull and metal sails. While one firm reproduced
ancient galleon, most mimicked American sailing vessels of the 19th
tury. Elaborate sidewheel steamers and even private launches and tug boats began to
manufactured in the early 1900s.

rains were next to make their appearance. A six-foot-long locomotive and tender
ld be had in 1883 from the Westervelt Company of New York City for $200. The
te firm offered a horse car, the forerunner of the trolley. Both were finely worked in
pper. There are also many flat sheet iron locomotives made by blacksmiths or metal
rkers.

lighly realistic automobiles appeared in the first decade of this century. Whether three
tensional or cut out, these vanes accurately depicted famous brands of the time, such
he Hupmobile, the Rolls-Royce, and the Cadillac. Other harder-to-locate forms of
nsportation include airplanes and the early high-wheeled bicycles known as "bone
shers."

triotic Motifs

Nineteenth-century Americans were imbued with a sense of patriotism, and this was
lected in the weathervanes they placed above their homes and public buildings. The
st ubiquitous of these, the eagle, is discussed above. Two other popular forms were
lumbia, the goddess of liberty, depicted holding an American flag in one hand and ges-
ing defiantly with the other, and the Statue of Liberty, many versions of which were
duced after it was installed in 1886.

ess common are flag vanes and those in the form
a Phrygian or Liberty cap, a soft cap popular dur-
; the American Revolution. Cannon-shaped vanes
d those consisting of a rifle and military cap may
o be thought of as falling within the patriotic cat-
ry.

Some unique homemade examples are also
own, including a forty-inch-high painted sheet
n Uncle Sam who appears to be thumbing his
se at the world and various eagle and flag combi-
tions. There is even a gilded aluminum represen-
ion of Paul Revere on horseback made in the
60s for the exclusive use of the Americana
tels. While not considered collectible by many,
se later vanes are already acquiring a following
ong enthusiasts who cannot pay the prices
manded for earlier examples.

STEER WEATHERVANE c. 1880-1910;
carved and painted wood; northeastern
United States. In considering this
powerful rendition of an important
draft animal, it is easy to understand
why collectors consider weathervanes
to be a major form of American
folk sculpture. *Private Collection.*

STEAM SAILING-SHIP WEATHERVANE
c. 1920-1940; painted wood, sheet tin,
and iron wire; Martha's Vineyard,
Massachusetts. Ship vanes are found frequently in coastal towns, where they were
made by whalers, fishermen, and sailors
in their spare time. *Private Collection.*

hirligigs

Whirligigs, often referred to as "wind toys," have a clouded history. One traditional story is that
first examples, in the form of toy soldiers with blade-like arms which spun madly in the wind,
re made to ridicule the Hessian troops employed by the English during the Revolutionary War.
other legend maintains that the first were created by the Amish people of Pennsylvania to pro-
e Sunday amusement for children who were forbidden to play with toys on the sabbath. There
not a shred of evidence to support either theory and very few American whirligigs seem to date
or to the last quarter of the 19th century, suggesting that they, like some other folk art items,
re a product of the nostalgia (known as Colonial Revival) which swept the country at the time
the 1876 Centennial. It is also possible that whirligigs derive from miniature versions of the
ropean windmill, made as children's playthings as far back as the 16th century and related to
common pinwheel toy. Some whirligigs found in England and on the Continent are clearly
lier than our examples.

n any case, like weathervanes, whirligigs are wind-powered and may serve as indicators of wind
ection. This function, though, is secondary to their main purpose, to serve as whimsical amuse-
nts for young and old.

There are four basic types, all usually cut and carved from wood or made from a combination
wood and metal. Most familiar is the single figure with blade-like or propeller arms which
n in the wind. Among the common forms are sailors (the Jolly Jack Tars still made for the
w England tourist trade), soldiers in 19th-century dress, Indians (both standing and in
oes), firemen, and
icemen. Harder to
d are witches and
n on horseback.
imals and birds are
o seen; ducks and
ese whose wings spin
dly in the breeze still
ace suburban lawns,
t far more interest-
z is the dog or squir-
whose tail flaps in
ne to the turning
des. There are also
bstantial numbers
patriotic whirligigs,
cluding Uncle Sam,

**BUGLER WITH FLAG
WHIRLIGIG** c. 1950; carved
and painted wood with iron,
tin, and cloth; New York. The
fixed flag, acting as a tail or
rudder, turns the whirligig into
the direction of the wind. This
causes the propeller to turn and
the bugler to march. *Courtesy
Museum of American Folk Art.*

NCLE SAM WHIRLIGIGS
84; carved and painted
od; Bill Duffy, New
rk. While Uncle Sam
a popular subject for
irligig makers, the
ack version is unusual.
llection of Joel and
ty Schatzberg.

ABRAHAM LINCOLN WHIRLIGIG 1978; carved and painted mahogany with tin, by Janice Fenimore (1924-), Madison, New Jersey. This appealing contemporay rendition of a well-known theme is the artist's first work in this form. *Private Collection.*

MAN SAWING WOOD WHIRLIGIG c. 1920-1930; painted saw-cut wood; northeastern United States. Wind toys like this one often depicted such varied farm activities as sawing wood, churning butter, or pumping water. *Private Collection.*

George Washington, Abraham Lincoln, the flag, and an early eagle with the seal of the Uni[ted] States on its breast and wing-shaped paddles.

Closely related are simple carved figures mounted with a small propeller. The propeller sp[ins] as the image (usually a wooden bird or animal) turns in the wind. These are essentially weath[er] vanes with a propeller.

More complex are whirligigs consisting of one or two figures which are geared so that [a] vagrant breeze will launch them on an endless, repetitive task: washing landry, sawing wood, [or] pumping the wheels of a bicycle. Such pieces were often made from directions provided in m[ag] azines of the 1930s and '40s such as *Popular Science*.

Far less common, much more difficult to construct, and rarely found in working order, are [the] Rube Goldberg-esque contraptions consisting of numerous figures which, when the wind blo[ws] will simultaneously launch into a variety of actions: playing cards, fishing, dancing, and the li[ke]. An outstanding example is the piece known as "Early Bird Gets The Worm," which is at [the] Museum of American Folk Art. Since the metal gears propelling these creations are easily rus[ted] by rain or damaged by high winds few have survived intact. They are, however, among the m[ost] extraordinary works of American folk art.

Almost all whirligigs are individually created pieces. Unlike weathervanes, many of the m[ost] desirable forms of which were made in shops or small factories, wind toys were usually tur[ned] out at home. There is, however, one exception. During the early 1900s several auto manuf[ac] turers produced mir[ia] ture metal whirlig[igs] as radiator cap or[na] ments. Among th[ese] now rare pieces (appropriately enou[gh] representations of tr[af] fic policemen!

DOG WHIRLIGIG
c. 1930-1940; cut and painted wood with iron wire; New Jersey. In this unusual form, a sitting dog wags its tail as the propeller turns in the wind. *Private Collection.*

MAN IN BOWL[ER] HAT WHIRLI[GIG]
c. 1880-1910; car[ved] and painted wo[od; northeastern Uni[ted] States. There are m[any] whirligigs, but [few] possess the dram[atic] sculptural power of [this] piece. *Private Collect[ion].*

CHAPTER 5

PUBLIC FOLK ART

ublic folk art or, rather, folk art publicly displayed has long been an American tradition and one with lengthy European antecedents. The carving and painting of public buildings was an ective way to impress upon the citizenry the power and majesty of the state. It also provided se who were taxed with some tangible evidence of where their money was going! In the United tes, eagles, flags, and national shields have always been preferred for the exteriors and interi- of courthouses, city halls, and similar edifices, while a much greater variety of carving and nting was deemed appropriate for commercial buildings and private residences.

s with portraiture, there was a class of artists and artisans eager to undertake the work. Early wspapers are filled with advertisements such as that of the carver and gilder, James Strachan, o advertised in *The New-York Gazette or The Weekly Post-Boy* for October 24, 1765, that he did sorts of House-Carvings in Wood or Stone, at the lowest Prices."

The commercial world offered even greater prospects for the painter or sculptor. Even in a coun- where literacy was rapidly becoming the norm, the tradition of the graphic trade sign continued, t as it does today. Newspapers of the 18th and 19th centuries are replete with advertisements ecting the buyer to " Henry Whiteman at the Sign of Buttons and Buckles, near the Oswego arket...Dennis MacReady Tobacconist at the sign of bladder of snuff and roll of tobacco" and the alebone cutter, David Philips, who worked at his house "opposite the Sign of the Three Pigeons." day's factory-produced signs may be generally less impressive, but they serve the same purposes—

BUILDING ARCHWAY DECORATION c. 1880-1915; pine with traces of old paint; Connecticut. An unknown country craftsman created this element to decorate a house or barn. Properly displayed, such fragments assume the aspect of folk sculpture. *Private Collection.*

ection and promotion. Already, ne of the more interesting early- h-century types, neon tubes and t Deco graphics, have become col- tible.

Humbler but reaching a wider dience was the art of the carousel. e tradition of carved and painted imals set on a moving platform ived in Europe from the East ring the 17th century. After the rousel became steam powered in e 1870s it was the focus of every nerican circus and traveling carni- , and carvers vied with one anoth- to produce the most spectacular rses and other animals.

VERTISING POSTER c. 1890-1900; ographed paper, printed in the rtheast for a patent medicine npany. Since they were practitioners "natural medicine", Native Ameri- s were often the subject of patent dicine advertising. *Author's Collection.*

77

Architectural Art

Only within the last decade or so has what we term architectural folk art become collectible began in New York City in the 1970s when artists and antique collectors began to salvage bits pieces of 19th-century buildings which were being destroyed in the name of "progress." W they salvaged varied greatly. There were strange medieval-looking gargoyles of granite, sa stone, or molded clay which decorated the rooftops and downspouts of turn-of-the-century t ements; there were turned oak and mahogany newel posts from earlier townhouses; and there a variety of moldings, pillars, and cornices that, while no longer in style, had a sculptural qua which enabled them to stand alone as works of art.

As interest spread these pieces were joined by louvered fan lights from rural barns and a vari of shutters, roof finials, and porch columns which originally graced suburban Victorian mansic Most bore several coats of weathered paint, the texture and faded color of which added to th folky charm.

Today such "accidental art" can be found incorporated into the architecture of everything fr contemporary apartments to converted hen-houses, or placed upon stands in white-walled roc and treated with almost the same respect accorded a Brancusi or a Calder.

Other more readily recognizable architectural pieces have long been of interest to folk art c lectors. Perhaps the most famous of these is the gate in the shape of the American flag which i the Museum of American Folk Art. This piece mirrors a strain of public patriotic express which continues today with the ubiquitous Uncle Sam mail box standards. Public buildings ere ed throughout the last century and much of this one also display such patriotic motifs as car eagles and figures of Columbia. Most interior examples (on lecterns, podiums, and the like) w of mahogany or oak; exterior adornment was of more humble pine and usually painted. As th buildings have been destroyed or modernized, s decoration has come into the hands of collectors.

The abundance of this material reflects the ecl tic Victorian taste, which incorporated a variety earlier architectural and sculptural motifs in bui ings which fairly dripped ornament, as well as presence of a large artisan class, skilled cabinetm ers, masons, and iron workers whose handiwork c tinues to appeal to connoisseurs.

A fascinating byproduct of architectural folk ar the commercial structure which, by its own sha serves to advertise the product or service offer Among the more common examples are stores in shape of a chicken which sell eggs and fowl, da product vendors operating out of milk-bottle-shap buildings, and even a car wash resembling a beach whale! While hardly collectible, these structures the closest thing to "folk architecture" one is likely encounter.

HEAD OF JUSTICE
c. 1875-1880; molded zinc; attributed to W.H. Mullins Company, Salem, Ohio. This head is a portion of a 10-foot-tall neoclassical sculpture. Works of this kind were made to adorn government offices and public buildings and are America's version of ancient Greek and Roman statuary. *Private Collection.*

LIBERTY WITH FLAG AND SWORD c. 1850-18 carved and painted wood; New Hampshire. Ima of the goddess of Liberty became increasin popular during the 19th century and could be fo in many forms and sizes. This fine example o decorated a boathouse. *Courtesy The Barenholtz Collect*

op Signs and Figures

: is not without reason that the painter William Williams, advertising in *The New-York Gazette* ' *the Weekly Mercury* on May 8, 1769, stated that he undertakes "painting in general, viz. tory, Portraiture, landskip [*sic.*], *sign painting*, lettering and gilding" (emphasis added). It was ly that a far better living could be derived at that time from painting tavern signs than from ting portraits or "landskips," and it had long been thus. Trade signs, painted on walls or ped from clay or stone, have been found in the buried ruins of ancient Pompeii and rculaneum; and they are frequently referred to in medieval literature. In this country, the ear- t references are to those that hung before the taverns which were found in towns and every few es along the "high roads" that connected major areas of settlement. A few bore a figure of chus, god of wine, but most were decorated with representations of important personages such george III or George Washington, or, of seemingly equal importance, of a great trotting horse Ethan Allen.

he value of such marks to identify a hostelry is reflected in the fact that tavern keepers fre- ntly referred to them in their advertisements, as did Nathaniel Ames of Massachusetts, whose l advertisement in *Ames' Almanack* advised

> **all Persons that travel the great Post-Road South West from Boston That I keep a house of Public Entertainment Eleven Miles from Boston at the sign of the Sun.**

lerchants had their own signs, many of long standing and readily recognizable to the passer- A knife or pair of scissors marked the cutler's shop; a red and white striped pole the barber, often doubled as local surgeon or bloodletter; a hand, the maker of gloves; and a stocking, hosier. The druggist had his mortar and pestle, the optician his pair of spectacles, the carpen- his saw, and, perhaps most graphic (and ominous) of all, the dentist his great white tooth.

o strong was the demand for trade signs and figures that many craftsmen in related fields turned r hands to this art. Included were painters, both of portraits and houses, carpenters, and at least pewterer, Paul Revere, who in 1770 carved and decorated a sign for Boston's Red Lion Inn.

he proliferation of elaborate and highly individualistic shop signs in 19th-century America was to more than literacy problems. A painted and gilded trade sign or a carved tobacconist's fig- not only indicated where a particular item might be bought, but also reflected the seller's sta- in the community. The more prominent a merchant, the larger his sign, to the extent that by late 1800s trade signs were becoming a nuisance. Hung from rods extending from buildings tanding on brackets in the street, they obstructed the right of way and, in a high wind, became enace to passersby (in the 1780s a pedestrian was killed outside John Duggan's tavern on Corn rt in Boston when a gale brought down the wood metal standard.) Trade signs even incited public rder, as in a Wyoming town where cigar store ians were removed from the street to prevent nken cowboys from shooting them up on rday nights.

he custom of self-promotion through trade signs figures still persists. Even in New York, the ld's most sophisticated city, there may still be

GUESTHOUSE SIGN c. 1900-1920; carved and turned, painted wood with iron; Manchester, Vermont. In the Art Nouveau style, this sign is typical of many that graced late Victorian guest cottages and guesthouses. *Courtesy Kelter-Malcé Antiques.*

CKMAKER'S SHOP SIGN c. 1870-1900; painted and ed cast iron and sheet tin; New York. It is said that the ds of clock signs such as this one are always set to show exact time of Lincoln's assassination. *Private Collection.*

found a fish store or two sporting its gilded salmon, and far downtown, a great carved pistol hangs above a shop that sells guns and ammunition. Moreover, signs constructed of neon tub or painted sheet metal and tubing (as with the common shoemaker's sign) remain popular as as collectible.

Collectors should bear in mind, though, that most of these signs were placed outside wh exposed to the weather, they suffered a variety of problems. Paint faded, wood cracked chipped, iron fittings rusted away. Few examples are found in original condition and, as it was custom to repaint signs or figures each spring, most will show several coats of paint.

An exception to this rule are the various signs and occasional small figures which were desig for use within a tavern, hotel or shop. Among the most interesting of these, from a historical spective, are the small painted boxes bearing the words " To Insure Promptness." Hostelry gu were expected to deposit a few coins for the staff in these receptacles; this gratuity gradually c to be referred to by the initials, "T.I.P."

Most popular of all trade figures are the cigar store Indians or tobacconists' figures which c were found outside every "segar-store." Introduced into England from the Americas by Sir Wa Raleigh, tobacco became a favored vice. And, since it was cultivated by Native Americans, rep sentations of these became associated with the weed.

Early 18th-century English versions reflected a lack of knowledge of Indian features, o depicting the bearer of the peace pipe and sheaf of tobacco as a black man wearing a feathe headdress and a kilt of tobacco leaves. American figures, which appeared soon after 1850, w more accurate. Chiefs, braves, and squaws were depicted, usually in traditional dress and arn with knife or tomahawk, as well as holding the traditional sheaf of tobacco.

CIGAR-STORE INDIAN
c. 1875-1890; carved and painted wood; by Samuel Robb (1851-1928), New York City. Robb was one of the best-known makers of trade figures and maintained a sizable shop in Manhattan for many years. *Courtesy Museum of American Folk Art.*

CIGAR-STORE INDIAN
c. 1910-1930; molded and painted chalk; northeastern United States. Small pieces like this were often given to tobacconists by their suppliers for display on counter tops. *Private Collecti*

CIGAR-STORE FIGURE
c. 1790-1830; carved and painted wood; England or the United States. This is the earliest form of the toba conist's trade sign. A black-amoor is seen clad in tobacc leaves and smoking a Dutch clay pipe. *Private Collection.*

SCULPTURAL EAGLE
c. 1860-1879; carved and
gilded pine; attributed to
John H. Bellamy, Kittery
Point, Maine. Bellamy
was a well-known carver
of figureheads, sternboards,
and pilot-house eagles.
The eagle shown here once
held an American flag in
its talons. *Private Collection.*

Between 1850 and 1920 thousands of these carved and painted figures were produced in merican shops. Ranging in size from two-foot counter figures to examples which towered well er six feet on their wheeled wooden platforms (so they could be hauled in at night), they depict- not only Indians but also such diverse figures as Uncle Sam, Punch, oriental potentates, fron- rsmen, famous actors and actresses, and even preachers.

Since some carvers signed their work, makers like Charles J. Dodge (1806-1886), Thomas V. ooks (1828-1895), and William Demuth (1835-1911), all of New York City, are well known to rious collectors. It was Demuth who revolutionized the field in the late 1800s by introducing st zinc figures which he described in his advertisements as being of a "more durable substance an wood, thus preventing cracking, which will sometimes occur in Wooden Figures, especially en exposed to the climate of our Southern States." Metal Indians may have lasted longer than eir wooden brothers (of whom it is estimated less than two ousand remain in existence), but they have never attained the ter's popularity among collectors.

CAROUSEL HORSE 1910;
carved and painted wood with
leather and metal, by Solomon
Stein and Harry Goldstein,
Brooklyn, New York. Carousel
figures were usually repainted
each season, so examples in original paint are rare.*Collection of The
Museum of American Folk Art, New
York. Gift of the City of New York,
Department of Parks and Recreation.*

arousel Figures

The carved and painted wooden horses and other animals ed on carousels or merry-go-rounds are another favored rm of folk sculpture. As far back as 500 AD Byzantine s-reliefs depicted people clinging to ropes attached to a volving overhead framework—the genesis of the carousel. By e 17th century this had evolved into a circular platform upon

HEART-IN-HAND LODGE SYMBOL c. 1870-1900;
rved, painted, and gilded wood; Pennsylvania.
he heart and hand, symbolizing generosity,
a mark of the Independent Order of Odd Fellows,
nale fraternal group. *Courtesy Alan Daniel.*

RESORT SIGN, "WOODTOP"
c. 1900-1930; painted sheet steel; New England or the Midwest. The amusing figure reflects the influence of early-20th-century cartoon art. *Courtesy Kelter-Malcé Antiques.*

which were mounted wooden horses, motive power be supplied by a living horse. When, in 1870, an Englishm Frederick Savage, provided steam power, the modern me go-round was born.

While also popular throughout Europe, no country had more carousels than the United States. As many as f thousand were operating at the turn of the century. To less than three hundred remain intact and functioning. individual animals, divided up among museums and col tors and carefully restored, serve to remind us of the h quality of carving and decorating that went into the mak craft. Though they appear to be solid pieces of wo carousel figures are actually made up of numerous small s tions glued and nailed together. These pieces combined form a hollow box-like structure, the exterior of which carved and given several coats of paint.

There are three basic types of American carousel a mal, each attributed to the school of an individual mak The first of these men, Gustav Dentzel, went into bu ness in Philadelphia in 1867. His son, William, sold business in 1928, at a time when many manufactur were shutting down. Dentzel animals showed refined f tures and great attention to muscular detail, with minin decorative embellishment. He and the makers who f lowed his lead are often referred to as the Philadelp school of carvers.

Charles I. D. Loof of Brooklyn entered the field in 18 remaining active until his death in 1918. Loof's less rea tic creations were highly ornate, with fanciful carving a painting enhanced by the addition of glass jewels and m rored trappings, in what came to be known as the Coney Island style.

Both Dentzel and Loof specialized in large, permanent merry-go-rounds with two or three r of animals. There was, however, a need for smaller, simpler, more durable carousels to be used carnivals and traveling circuses. These were supplied by Charles W.F. Dare of New York C who, in 1884, originated the Country Fair style. He was succeeded by the Herschell-Spilln company which produced the greatest variety of American carousel animals, including hors pigs, zebras, sea serpents, cats, dogs, roosters, goats, deer, ostriches, and even frogs.

Among these many beasts, the most desirable are those which were made for the outside rows a merry-go-round as these, being most visible, were most lavishly decorated. Moreover, the ou side of each animal, called the "view" or "romance" side, was always more heavily decorated. Ot portions of the carousel structure, such as the case for the pipe organ or the rounding boards wh concealed the machinery, were also decorated. These, too, are of interest to some collectors.

Since carousels were generally repainted at the beginning of each new season, figures are rar found in original paint. Most collectors of carousel animals, unlike those who collect other ty of folk art, generally prefer to strip their finds, restore the frames when necessary, and then co pletely repaint them in appropriate colors.

UNCLE SAM CANDY CONTAINER c. 1930-1950; lithographed paper over cardboa United States. Made for the Fanny Farmer candy company, these receptacles w often given as favors at Fourth of July parties. *Courtesy Helaine and Burton Fendelm*

TRADE CARD
c. 1880-1900;
lithographed
cardboard, Lowell,
Massachusetts.
The use of half-clad
mermaids on this
card is quite unusual
for the staid Victorian
era. *Private Collection.*

CHAPTER 6

NAUTICAL ART

No class of Americans created a greater variety of folk art than did sailors and those, such as ship carvers, who worked for them. Despite the hardships of life at sea, mariners often had long periods of inactivity which they filled with the practice of highly personal crafts such as the making of scrimshaw carvings and the building of ship models.

Ship builders and owners were concerned with the appearance of their vessels almost as much as with their seaworthiness. A carved figurehead, often accompanied by additional decorative elements such as sternboard, gangways, and taffrail, was a requirement for a ship of any substantial size. Indeed, no less a personage than John Hancock, in charge of the nation's newly created Marine Committee in 1776, admonished a builder of frigates to

> let the heads and galleries for the ships be neatly carv'd and Executed, I leave the Device
> [figurehead] to you, but by all means let ours be as good, handsome, strong & as early
> completed as any building here in Philadelphia.

This pride in ownership and appearance was further manifested by the proliferation of artists who specialized in paintings of ships, both naval and commercial. Employed by merchants, owners of shipping lines, and captains of sailing vessels, these painters created a category of folk art that is highly sought-after today.

Finally, sailors like all travelers bought souvenirs. In the West Indies they purchased "sailors' valentines," shell work creations housed in mahogany cases and featuring a touching expression directed to home and family. Shell-covered boxes and other receptacles were also popular trinkets, as well as coconuts carved in the manner of scrimshaw.

Scrimshaw

The chief leisure activity of the American sailor was scrimshaw work, the incising or carving of bits of ivory, usually taken from whales. While primarily a whaleman's pastime (since they had the readiest access to raw material), scrimshandering, as it was called, was practiced by any sailors who could obtain a supply of ivory, as well as by "landlubbers."

So prevalent was the hobby in the 19th century that it was often

"JAGGING WHEEL" OR
PIE CRIMPER c. 1830-1850;
carved and pierced whalebone
and ivory; New England.
Featuring hinged "teeth" for
piercing crust to allow juice to
escape, this is one of the more
complex examples known and
is decorated with over a dozen
hearts. *Courtesy Barbara Johnson.*

SCRIMSHAW WHALE'S TOOTH
c. 1820-1840; incised carbon-
ized figure on whale ivory;
New England. Such stylish
female figures as this one were
often copied from illustrations
in the women's magazines
of the period. *Private Collection.*

SWIFT OR WOOL WINDER
c. 1840-1850; turned and carved whale bone and ivory with silk ribbons; New Bedford, Massachusetts. These complex devices were used to measure skeins of yarn. This example features a fist-shaped table clamp. *Courtesy Barbara Johnson.*

mentioned in print, as in the log book entry for May 20, 1826 of the brig, *By Chance*— "all ha employed scrimshonting"— and the 1842 journal of Captain William M. Davis in which he notes t

in scrimshoning we carve and work much on the ivory of whale's teeth, and by inlaying with pearl some beautiful objects are wrought.

Three types of material were employed in scrimshandering: whale or walrus teeth, baleen stiff, horn-like material which was used in making flexible objects like women's corset stays "busks" and hoop skirt supports, and pan bone taken from the whale's jaw.

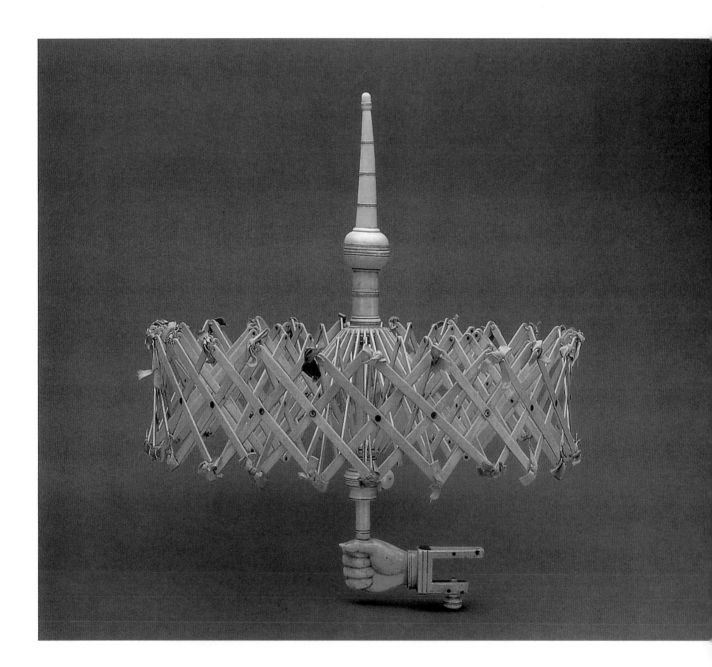

SCRIMSHAW SHOWCASE dated 1855; mahogany with whale ivory, br silver, and velvet; by William Chappell, New Bedford, Massachusetts. Chapp a crew member of the ship *Saratoga*, made this for his captain. *Courtesy Sothe*

On teeth and pan bones were incised, with a needle or other sharp object, various pictures and messages for loved ones at home. Popular themes were attractive and stylish women, patriotic figures, historic sea battles, and, of course, whaling scenes. While a few gifted artists did freehand work, the majority would lay a dampened illustration from a magazine such as *Godey's Lady's Book* over the tooth, then carefully prick out its outline with a needle. The holes would then be joined together and the outline filled in with red or blue ink or lamp black.

Bone was also carved into a variety of useful objects such as pie crimpers or jagging wheels, elaborate swifts for measuring yarn, cane and umbrella handles, openwork baskets, needle cases, clothespins, ditty boxes, bobbins, bird cages, toys, and such nautical tools as fids, knife handles, seam rubbers, rulers, bodkins, and the whale stamps used to record the capture of a leviathan in the ship's log. Whale bone was also often combined with exotic woods like mahogany, teak, and ebony in the manufacture of items such as rolling pins, dippers, serving trays, and storage boxes in many shapes and sizes.

Authentic scrimshaw can bring high prices at auction (several of the "Susan's Teeth" made aboard the bark *Susan* of Sag Harbor, Long Island in the 1820s have sold for over $20,000). However, fakes and reproductions have been made for decades, and collectors must be extremely cautious.

SCRIMSHAW WHALE TEETH
c. 1830-1840; ivory teeth with incised decoration filled with lamp black; New England. Matching pairs of teeth, such as these patriotic examples, are rare. *Courtesy Sotheby's.*

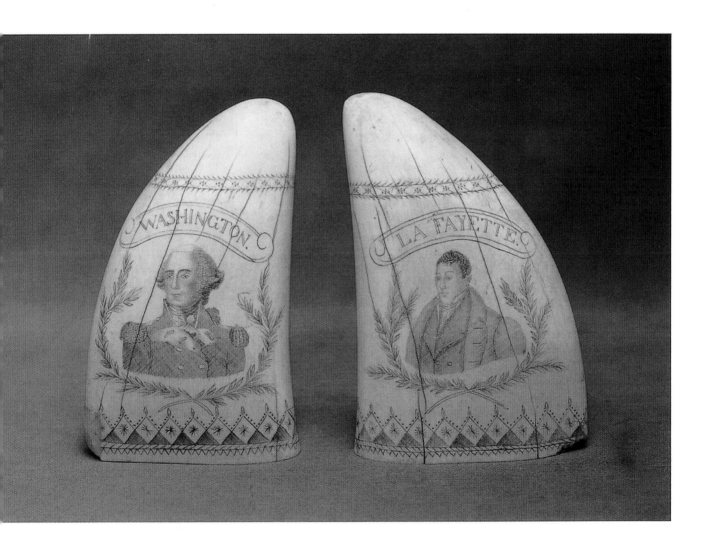

"JAGGING WHEEL" OR PIE CRIMPER c. 1850; carved whale bone and ivory; Nantucket, Massachusetts. Pie crimpers were among the many tokens of affection made by sailors for their wives or sweethearts. *Courtesy Barbara Johnson.*

SHIP'S FIGUREHEAD
c. 1865-1875; carved and
painted pine; Maine. This
stern figure is believed to
be a representation of
President Ulysses S. Grant.
Courtesy Frank Maresca

▶pe Work

▪Rope work was another nautical pastime. ▪ chest handles or beckets were woven of ▪rse line as were floor mats, some the size ▪ small carpets. These mats were often ▪ted or interlaced in a complex manner ▪lecting the sailor's skill with knots, an ▪lity most frequently displayed by mount-▪; various examples on a polished ▪hogany board.

▶p Models

▪hip models were made by sailors, of ▪rse, but they were also created by others ▪o never sailed the seas. There are three ▪eral categories to be considered: free-▪nding models, shadow box vessels, and ▪ps in bottles. All have been produced ▪r a long period of time, and are still ▪ng made.

▪ree-standing models are designed to be ▪niature replicas of full-sized ships. Some early ones were actually builder's models used as a ▪nstruction guide. Most, though, were made for pleasure. A Maine seaman wrote to his wife in ▪51 to tell her that

> I have whittled a ship and a lighthouse for you with a pilot boat putting out to sea. It is
> a copy of the A.C. Watson....She is a sweet little schooner.

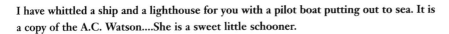

▪The best of these models are built to scale and include all the important details found on a com-▪rable vessel: planked hulls, life boats, gun ports, anchors, cabins, and, most important, proper ▪ging. Size varies greatly. Some examples are five feet long; most are under two feet. A few of ▪ finer specimens have been mounted under glass cases to protect their fragile sails. Particularly ▪zed are "prisoner-of-war" models—usually made from discarded soup bones—which were the ▪duct of French, English, or American sailors imprisoned during the wars of the late 18th and ▪ly 19th centuries.

▪Shadow box models were made both at sea and in many seafaring towns along the Atlantic coast. ▪ey consist of a simplified hull with rigging, which is cut in half and mounted against a wood-▪ background painted to resemble an ocean scene. This was then set within a deep, glass-cov-▪ed shadow box frame. Such models were rarely built to scale, and they are frequently inaccu-▪ely rigged. However, they may be wonderfully folky with their brightly painted ground and ▪y-like ship. Larger examples may incorporate several vessels and a shoreline built up with model ▪uses, trees, and the requisite lighthouse.

▪Less frequently seen are dioramas: sailors in a longboat in pursuit of a whale, a shipboard scene, ▪ a dramatic hand-to-hand battle between naval boarding parties. Since these involve the carv-▪g of human figures, they were usually undertaken by only the most skilled craftsmen.

▪Perhaps the most generally popular of all nautical art is the ship in a bottle. Designed to baf-▪ (how did they ever get that thing in there?) as well as amuse, these miniature models have ▪en made at least since the mid-19th century. Earlier examples are mounted within hand-▪own bottles. Size is determined by the available bottle; most fit within a quart-sized or small-▪ container. The vessel (or vessels) within is mounted on a painted plaster sea and frequently ▪es at anchor before a small harbor or port town on a hill, built of plaster and wood. Many ▪productions are available: some are made in the traditional way, others of incredibly delicate ▪own glass crafted in Italy.

MODEL OF U.S.S. CONSTITUTION c. 1920-1940; carved and painted wood with cloth, thread, and iron wire; New England. The *Constitution* is among the most popular subjects for ship modelers. *Private Collection.*

Ship Carving

Carved bow-mounted ships' figureheads come from a tr dition of great antiquity. They were found on Roman a Egyptian vessels, and are related to the dragon-like prows the Viking whaleboats. No doubt the earliest were design to strike fear into the hearts of superstitious foes, but pr tige eventually became a more important consideration finely-carved figurehead demonstrated the wealth of t ship's owner.

The earliest American examples appear to have been in t form of a lion, reflecting traditional British iconography. bill submitted in 1689 by the carvers Edward Budd a Richard Knight of Boston for the sloop, *Speedwell*, referr to a "Lyon," and "a neat carv'd Lyon's Head fit for a ship about 400 Hogsheads Burthen" was offered for sale in 17 by a Maryland firm.

Other animal forms such as horse heads gradually becar popular, but by the mid-1700s these were largely replaced representations of humans. Simeon Skillin (1716-1778) a his sons, John and Simeon, Jr., among the most high regarded of these early carvers, produced a wide range of f ures including Spanish *dons* or cavaliers, Venus, Engli heroes like the Black Prince, "Old Put" (the devil), and ev a Portuguese king. American sculptors of the 19th centu preferred women, including semi-nude figures, as well as variety of personages including statesmen, politicians, an of course, Uncle Sam.

The gradual introduction during the second half of t 19th century of steel-hulled vessels made installation of f ureheads more difficult; and when the United States Navy, 1907, ordered them removed from its ships, the traditi came to an end. A substantial number of examples have su vived in museums and private collections.

The pilot house eagle was another important form of na tical carving, a dramatic representation of the national b mounted atop the small building in which the helmsm stood. Relief- carved eagles also decorated the paddle bo of American steamships and the tops of masts. The great carver of these eagles was John Bellamy (1836-1914) Kittery Point, Maine.

Less often seen are the large and elaborate sternbo carvings decorated with complex floral and figural moti gangway boards that decorated the entrance to the ship, a cat heads, traditionally carved in the form of a lion fac which served as cranes in raising the anchors. Because many of the old sailing ships were broken up without rega to the artistry of their carved work, little of this subsidia folk sculpture has survived.

Ship Paintings

The United States has a long tradition of nautical paintin Among the earliest examples are the small reverse gla paintings of naval battles of the Revolution and War of 181

SHIP'S FIGUREHEAD
c. 1830-1850; carved and painted wood; Portland-Boston area. Women were a popular subject of figurehead art for sailors who were often away from wives or sweethearts for several years at a time. *Private Collection.*

THE SARAH PASSING FLUSHING dated 1849; reverse painted oils on glass; China. Chinese port artists often painted views of American vessels, in this case a clipper ship passing Flushing, New York. Large numbers of Chinese paintings depicting American subjects were exported to the United States during the 19th century. *Courtesy Museum of American Folk Art.*

SHADOWBOX MODEL c. 1910-1930; carved and painted wood with painted plaster sea and watercolor sky, set within a shadowbox of wood and glass; New York. Folk art using maritime subjects, such as this American steamship, was often the work of sailors who used their spare time to create a wide range of objects. *Private Collection.*

These usually depict one-on-one conflicts between a ship of the infant American fleet and one o the sea-tested Royal navy. Inspiring great patriotic fervor, representations of such victoriou engagements as those between the *Constitution* and the *Guerriere* and the *United States* and th *Macedonian* were frequently featured on the glass tablets which adorned many Federal mirrors an clock faces. Ironically, these folk adaptations were usually based on British prints. Having lost th battles, the English won the market!

The earliest known portrait of an individual American sailing ship is that of the *Bethel* of Bostor painted in the mid- 18th century, but the great majority of such paintings date to the period afte 1850. By this time our commercial fleet had expanded tremendously, and clipper ships flying th stars and stripes dominated international trade. The proud builders, owners, and captains of thes vessels wanted to preserve them on canvas, and a small group of artists set about to satisfy thei wishes. Most of these painters worked in seaports along the Atlantic coast where both patrons an subject matter were readily available.

Many of these men were academically trained, but there were also some successful artists work ing in the folk tradition. Chief among these were Antonio Jacobsen (1850-1921) and the broth ers James (1815-1897) and John (??-1856) Bard. Jacobsen, Danish by birth, began to paint in Ne

HARBOR SCENE
c. 1950-1960; oil on mason-
ite; by Earl Cunningham
(1893-1965), St. Augustine,
Florida. Cunningham, who
spent his life as a sailor,
painted over 500 works,
most of which were
seascapes. *Private Collection.*

U.S.S. MERCIDITA
c. 1870-1890; charcoal
and ink on paper. The
naval vessel, shown under
way, is a transitional ship
combining sail and steam
propulsion. *Private Collection.*

York City in 1875. He later established a studio in Hoboken, New Jersey where he turned out hundreds of paintings on canvas and artist's board. These ranged from clippers and other sailing ships through sail-steamers, steamships, and yachts, to the small harbor tugs which handled the larger vessels. Famous for his attention to detail, Jacobsen earned a good living catering to the shipping trade of New York Harbor.

The Bard brothers were even more prolific. They worked together in New York City for about twenty years, and following John's death, James continued on into the 1890s. He alone is credited with over a thousand paintings, about half of which have survived. Somewhat less proficient than Jacobsen, his work is characterized by naive backgrounds and tiny, crude human figures set against blue skies and sparkling seas.

Though born in the same era, the folk painter J.O.J. Frost (1852-1928) of Marblehead, Massachusetts did not begin his career as a nautical painter until 1923, when a visitor asked him for a sketch recreating a scene of his youth as a sailor. During the next five years Frost turned out some eighty oils of nautical topics, and he is now regarded as one of the most important 20th century folk artists.

Due to the great demand for nautical paintings, the work of Jacobsen, the Bards, and even Frost has largely been priced out of the range of the average collector. However, there are many other little-known or unknown painters of the same period whose work is both interesting and relatively inexpensive.

Sailors' Souvenirs

Sailors were also tourists, and though not made in this country many of the objects they brou·
back from their travels have become part of the American folk heritage. Captains, mates, ·
other well-heeled members of the crew purchased "port paintings," done on canvas or glass
native artists, depicting ships, crew members, or the "hongs" or Chinese trading posts. Fr
England wealthier sailors brought embroidered wool pictures featuring American sailing vess
and from Japan and China more finely made embroideries with silver and gold thread, feath
work, and paintings on silk. These often had a small pocket into which could be inserted a ·
ture of the seaman or a loved one.

Crew members settled for a less expensive class of mementos such as the "sailor's valentine.
shell mosaic produced in the West Indies. A mahogany box, usually octagonal and often wit·
hinged cover, was filled with vari-colored sea shells set under glass in a floral or geometric patt·
(hearts were especially popular). Worked into the design would be a homely phrase such·
"Remember Me," "To My Love," or "Souvenir of Barbadoes." Particularly popular today are d·
ble valentines with two mosaics hinged together; these often sell for over a thousand dollars.

Shells were also used to decorate a variety of useful objects including small boxes and pict·
frames. A particular favorite with seamen was an anchor-shaped, shell-covered wooden ·
plaque, often with a cloth-covered pin cushion attached. Many of these were made in the Brit·
Isles where they were offered to tourists at beach resorts, but they were also made for sailors st·
ping at ports in such diverse spots as the Philippines and South Africa.

Large, heavy shells such as the conch and cowrie were engraved by grinding away the ou·

layer of shell, leaving a pictorial relief set against the mother-of-pearl of the interior. Most of these were produced in Italy. Similar work was done in the warmer climes employing the ivory nut or palm tree seed. After the rough outer bark was peeled away this hard, rich brown nut could be engraved with nautical scenes such as the traditional "sailor's farewell." In an interesting variation, the two small depressions at one end of the nut were fitted with glass eyes and a face carved about them, giving the object some resemblance to a small, weasel-like animal.

The sand bottle, a glass vial or bottle filled with simple layers of different colored sands or with a picture built up from vari-hued earths was another unusual sailors' novelty. These were being made by the 1840s on the Isle of Wight, and later in the century seafarers visiting Chile obtained examples in rare colors produced from the nitrate bearing sands of that country. Sand bottle art is still being created today, especially in the American west, but it is no longer strictly nautical in content.

Finally, there was straw work, a form of marquetry practiced by sailors, especially prisoners of war. This involved decorating boxes, tea caddies, picture frames, and even small pieces of furniture with plaited strips of colored straw glued to the surface in various designs, both geometric and pictorial. The best of this ware was produced in the early 19th century by French seamen; the art was continued into the 1900s by Austrian craftsmen.

SAILOR'S DITTY BOX
c. 1810-1830; baleen with pine top and bottom; scrimshaw decoration; Nantucket, Massachusetts. Baleen, a flexible whale membrane, was used to shape this oval storage box. *Courtesy Barbara Johnson.*

CHAPTER 7

THE WORLD IN MINIATURE

A rt often imitates life, and this is especially true of folk art, the practitioners of which frequently enjoy creating miniaturized versions of the larger world around them. In some cases the objects produced serve a very practical purpose, as with the decoys made to lure ducks and shorebirds as well as fish. More often the pieces are purely decorative. The molded gypsum figurines known as chalkware were made "for pretty" to be displayed as decorations in otherwise drab houses. This was also true of the small toys and figurines made in earthenware and stoneware by American potters. On the other hand, miniature books of marble or slate were produced as gifts or novelties, as were the rustic wooden objects often referred to as "wacky wood." Whatever their original purpose, all these objects are now part of the folk art pantheon.

Decoys

The gregarious nature of waterfowl makes it practical to lure them within hunting range by using either other live ducks or artificial decoys made to resemble their living brethren. At least a thousand years ago Native Americans, the Tule Eaters of the southwestern United States, employed duck-like lures of bound reeds and feathers for this purpose.

By the 1850s American hunters were using duck and shorebird decoys carved and painted in a realistic manner, made either by themselves or by local craftsmen. Since they were easily lost or damaged by bird shot, few of these early examples have survived. However, the great popularity of hunting over the past century has led to the production of so many decoys that examples from this period are the most readily available of all American folk sculpture.

Waterfowl decoys fall into two broad categories: ducks and shorebirds. The duck may be further subdivided into floaters and stickups, which are mounted on a rod

MAN ON BICYCLE c. 1893-1920; carved and painted wood with iron and tin; northeastern United States. The date 1839 may relate to the development of the bicycle. In that year a Scottish blacksmith, Kirkpatrick MacMillan, fashioned a two-wheel vehicle that may have looked like this. *Private Collection.*

MALLARD DRAKE DECOY c. 1930-1950; carved and painted cedar; New York. Clearly, a sophisticated carver has taken care to insure that his piece closely resembles a living bird. *Private Collection.*

FISH DECOY c. 1930-1950; carved and painted pine; Minnesota. Few fish decoys are as well carved as this representation of a white sucker, a common forage fish. *Private Collection.*

CANADA GOOSE DECOY c.1920-1930; carved and painted pine and cedar; Connecticut. A true folk decoy, the goose's body consists of nothing more than a section of painted log. *Private Collection.*

YELLOWLEGS DEC c. 1890-1910; carved a painted wood; Long Isla New York. Since hunti for shorebirds or "pee was outlawed early in 20th century, examples this type of decoy are u common. *Private Collecti*

for planting in the ground. Shorebirds, which mimic the small birds like yellowlegs, curlews, an plovers which feed along the tidal flats, are always made as stickups.

Authentic duck decoys are far more common than their shorebird counterparts, as hunting th latter was outlawed early in the 20th century. As a result, thousands of decoys shorebird deco were thrown away or burned as kindling wood.

While most decoys—including the most collectible—are of carved and painted pine or ceda they are also found in other materials. Some are made of canvas stretched over a wire frame, oth ers have balsa wood bodies, and there are even cast iron examples which were mounted on raft Shorebird decoys are found in painted, stamped tin as well as wood. Both types can be either full three-dimensional or flat silhouettes.

Not all decoys were made in the form of ducks or shorebirds. Birds such as swans and sea gull which are not hunted for food, were mimicked in the belief that these "confidence decoys" wou encourage huntable birds to approach. Pigeon and crow decoys were also made, as were ow designed not to attract but to repel birds which attacked crops.

Decoys are tremendously popular not only with folk art enthusiasts but also among hunters an decoy specialists who collect no other folk objects. As a result prices have escalated in the la decade, with a few examples bringing over $100,000. The more valuable items tend to be tho made by famous carvers like Nathan Cobb, Charles "Shang" Wheeler, and A. Elmer Crowe Still, a finely carved and beautifully painted but unidentified bird will quickly find a home.

The fish decoys used in ice fishing on the northern lakes are a related collectible. Fish deco are also usually made of carved and painted wood, generally weighted to keep them upright, an mounted with tin or leather fins. Some are carefully painted to resemble actual fish such as suc ers, sturgeon, and sunfish. Most, however, are decorated in garish colors unknown in nature b thought to attract game fish.

The fish decoy, which does not have hooks, is lowered on a line through a hole in the ice an jiggled up and down to create the impression of a living meal for a large fish. When the predat approaches the fisherman attempts to jab it with an iron trident-like spear.

Though most are small (less than ten inches long) and crudely made, fish decoys have attrac ed a cult-like following of enthusiasts who seek out the relatively few examples by respecte carvers like Oscar Peterson (1877-??) of Cadillac, Michigan. There are also a substantial numb of factory-made specimens produced by firms which make fishing tackle. One of the major prol lems in the field is th vast number of contem porary reproduction which are often offere to the unsuspecting old, used decoys.

Also very collectib are the wrought iro spears used in ice fish ing and for spearin eels and freshwate fish, usually at nigh with aid of a spotligh Fish spears are ofte fine examples of th blacksmith's craft wit delicately shaped fa like blades terminatin in hooked barb Mounted on a woode block or against a wal they become fo sculpture.

PAIR OF MALLARDS
c. 1940-1960; carved and painted pine with cast-lead legs and feet; New England. Decorative decoys such as these miniatures are popular with many collectors. *Private Collection.*

halkware

Among the most charming of American folk sculptures are all figures cast from plaster or gypsum, allowed to dry, and en painted in bright colors (typically red, yellow, blue, green, d black). Long associated with Pennsylvania, most either orig- ated in Europe or were made here by immigrant craftsmen. iladelphia newspapers carried mid-19th century advertise- ents by several Italian workers who produced such wares, car- ing their molds, plaster, and paints on their backs from town to wn.

Considering how fragile they were, a surprising number of old alk figures have survived. A major collection at the Museum of merican Folk Art in New York City contains dozens of figures, to twenty-four inches tall, in several different designs.

Birds were a particular Pennsylvania favorite; doves, swans, osters, parrots, and pairs of lovebirds were particularly popular. nong the many animals are lions, pigs, horses, squirrels, deer, ats, sheep, rabbits, and several types of dogs. Cats were so pop- ar that some of the largest examples of chalkware were in this rm. Human figures are less common and tend toward the ctorian sentimentality of little girls with doves, mothers and ildren, or sprightly "bloomer girls." Rarities include the fire- in in full uniform with his axe upon his shoulder and George ashington on horseback.

Some of the earliest examples of chalkware are in the form of igious plaques and figures. These include scenes of the last pper and the holy family; angel statues in various sizes were o popular. Church models, among the largest of chalkware eces, were probably designed for Christmas displays, as were e rare figures of Saint Nick.

Uncommon types of chalkware include watch safes (stands in e form of classical facades which were used to convert a pock- watch into a small clock) and garnitures in pairs for mantel display. The latter were usually made the shape of pineapples (symbolizing hospitality) or baskets of fruit and vegetables (another sign welcome and bounty).

Some pieces of chalkware were given slots and used as penny banks, while smaller birds and ani- ls were sometimes mounted on a fabric and wood bellows so that when pressed down they ide a noise (hence their name, "squeak toys"). The nodder, a piece with its head attached to its dy by a steel spring or wire loop so that it would bob about when touched, was another inter- ing variation. A figure of a talkative old woman is typical of the type, though animal nodders e more common.

While most chalkware is found in and around Pennsylvania, some appears to have made its way st. In his *Adventures of Huckleberry Finn*, Samuel Clemens has Huck describe a house with a antel upon which sat "a big outlandish parrot on each side of the clock made up of something e chalk and painted up gaudy."

There is no doubt that most chalkware was intended for such decorative use, perhaps serving in ace of more expensive Staffordshire earthenware mantelpiece figures. On the other hand, both e form and the decoration of chalk owes more to continental Europe than to the British Isles.

Chalkware went out of style and production in the late 19th century, but it reappeared in the 20s in the form of prizes given away at carnival and circus games of chance. These pieces, which e still made, may be distinguished from 19th-century examples by the fact that the earlier pieces e always hollow. Carnival chalk, though also cast, is solid and heavy, and is more likely to be inted in pastel shades and sprinkled with bits of silver or gold glitter.

CHALKWARE DOG
c. 1880-1900; molded
and painted plaster of
Paris; Pennsylvania.
Dogs, modeled on English
Staffordshire mantelpiece
figures, were a popular
subject for the makers
of chalkware novelties.
Private Collection.

Long ignored as gaudy and of too-recent vintage, carnival chalk is now eagerly sought out [by] certain collectors attracted by the variety of figures to be found. There are of course, the us[ual] animals, especially dogs and horses, a few birds, and even a fish or two. But the big attractions [are] the humans, everyone from flappers and Indian chiefs to movie icons like Betty Boop and Cha[rlie] Chaplin. Cartoon characters such as Mickey Mouse and Donald Duck are of equal popularity.

Another source of appeal is cost. While chalk figures from the 1800s regularly sell for $200 a[nd] up, carnival ware is seldom priced above $50, other than for rare cartoon or movie figures. Th[ere] is a great quantity available, so much that one need not settle for damaged pieces—a sim[ilar] undamaged example will be along soon enough.

CHALKWARE CARNIVAL FIGURE c. 1920-1930; molded and painted plaster. Unlike 19th century examples, these inexpensive novelties are not hollow. *Private Collection.*

MICKEY MOUSE STILL BANK c. 1930-1940; painted composition with sheet tin base, marked "Walt Disney Crown", United States. Banks made of plaster-like composition material were fragile. Few have survived. *Courtesy The Margaret Woodbury Strong Museum.*

ural Ceramics

Miniature figures were also produced from ceramic materials. From the 18th through the late h centuries American potters made everything from toys to reproductions of Staffordshire fig- nes in redware or the more durable gray stoneware. As early as 1660 the Manhattan potter, ck Claesen, was described as making "clay toys," and throughout the 1800s Pennsylvania tsmen turned out such objects as redware whistles, tops, marbles, penny banks, and various iature versions of jugs, crocks, and pitchers. Most of these were shaped by hand, making them e one-of-a-kind pieces of folk art. Some were left unglazed, others covered with a shiny lead ze, and a limited number were splashed with slip in several colors.

xamples in stoneware covered with a clear salt glaze or a rich brown Albany slip include rstops in the form of lions, dogs or classical figures, and a group of bizarre jugs, most from the na, Illinois pottery (c. 1859-1896), which are covered with snakes and other unpleasant crea- es (a not-too-subtle reference to delirium tremens and a plea for abstinence from hard liquor). other product of this factory was a group of small whiskey tasters in the form of pigs, the backs which were incised with the route of an Illinois railway line.

)ne of the most interesting and folky forms, made both in stoneware and redware, is the e jug: a jug-shaped vessel, the front of which has been sculpted into a human likeness, often h white porcelain teeth and eyes. Most of these originate in the South, and some have ued that the form shows African influence. There is no doubt, however, that similar pieces re being made in Europe as far back as the 1700s. Whatever the case, numerous contem-

EARTHENWARE VESSELS c. 1880-1900; glazed stone- ware; Missouri. This group of pieces, from various potteries, includes two so- called snake jugs, a lamb, a basket, and an owl-shaped doorstop. *Private Collection.*

COW CREAMER
c. 1849-1858; molded Rockingham glazed yellowware; Bennington, Vermont. The piece was filled through a hole in the back, and cream flowed through the mouth when poured. *Private Collection.*

PIG BANK
c. 1870-1920; Albany slip-glazed stoneware; Ohio. The body of this folky pig was shaped from a jug. *Private Collection.*

porary potters throughout the South are reproducing these popular jugs today, and they are a favorite tourist purchase.

Figural forms were also made in Rockingham and yelloware. The famous United States Pottery (1847-1858) at Bennington, Vermont turned out a great variety of figures in the brown-splashed yellow earthenware called Rockingham, including cow-shaped creamers, whiskey bottles which looked like books, men in long robes, and mantel ornaments in the form of lions, deer and cows. These were customarily cast in molds but often had hand- applied decorative elements. Figural yelloware is less common, but among the known examples are banks shaped like pears or barrels, a rare cow creamer, and numerous food molds designed to turn out everything from fish to fowl.

MECHANICAL ARTILLERY BANK c. 1892-1910; painted cast iron with steel spring; by W. J. Shepard Hardware Company, Buffalo, New York. A coin placed in the cannon barrel may be fired into a slot in the bank. *Courtesy The Margaret Woodbury Strong Museum.*

ROOSTER STILL BANK c. 1920-1935; painted and gilded cast iron; the Hubley manufacturing Company, Lancaster, Pennsylvania. The term "still" bank refers to banks which have no mechanical parts. These hollow containers for the saving of coins were made in many forms that included a variety of architectural, animal, and human shapes. *Courtesy The Margaret Woodbury Strong Museum.*

HOUSE STILL BANK paten
1892; painted cast ir
northeastern United Sta
This safe is in the form
Gothic cottage, a popular build
style of the period. *Courtesy
Margaret Woodbury Muse*

POODLE DOORSTOP
c. 1860-1880; molded
Rockingham glazed ware;
Ohio. Other known
Rockingham animal
forms include deer, lions,
and cows. *Private Collection.*

Miniatures in Stone

The material a folk artist employs often reflects his primary occupation. In New England, particularly Vermont and New Hampshire, the men who worked in the quarries cutting building stone developed a very personal type of folk art: they shaped miniature books of marble or red or black slate. Usually no more than four by five inches in size, these were incised with titles, the names of recipients, or Victorian motifs such as a bird or bunch of flowers. From their form and size it seems likely that these uncommon items were designed to serve as paperweights.

These craftsmen also produced larger pieces, multicolored bricks and octagonal balls which were either made from several stones of contrasting colors or polychrome painted. Their bulk and weight indicates that they were probably designed as doorstops.

STONE DOORSTOPS OR PAPERWEIGHTS
c. 1870-1890; left, polychrome painted marble;
right, assemblage of vari-colored marble
sections; both Vermont. *Private Collection.*

WATCH HUTCH c. 1880-1910;
turned and carved marble;
Vermont. A watch placed in the
round hole would serve as a miniature
mantel clock. *Private Collection.*

Wooden Whimsies

Another unusual and distinct group of small items appeared during the early 20th century. Reflecting the rustic craze of the period, which included everything from hunting lodges and rooms full of twig or horn furniture to Native American crafts and costume, these objects included handmade wooden pitchers, mugs, and bottles, many of which were decorated with declomania representations of Native Americans or slogans etched with a hot iron. The miniature wishing well, a round well with overhead crane from which a bucket was suspended, was an especially popular item. Most of these were designed to be sold as souvenirs, and they bore sentiments like "Welcome to Lake George " or "Souvenir of the Poconos" or the name of the town or historic site where they were being sold.

Known today among dealers and collectors as "wacky wood," these modestly-priced pieces have gained a substantial audience aware of their handmade status and distinct local provenance. It is possible, for example, to assemble a collection focusing solely on a particular resort area such as New York's Adirondack Mountains or the Blue Ridge area of Virginia.

Following page:
CHRISTMAS TREE ORNAMENTS c. 1920-1940; a group of painted blown glass ornaments; Germany. The finest and most complex ornaments were handmade in Germany prior to World War II and were collected and cherished by many American families. *Courtesy Helaine and Burton Fendelman.*

FATHER TIME c. 1900-1910; carved and painted wood with human hair and brass accessories; New York. The purpose of this piece is unknown, though originally the articulated arm allowed the figure to ring the bell. *Courtesy The Museum of American Folk Art.*

NOAH'S ARK c. 1900-1920; carved and saw-cut painted wood; Germany. Because of its religious nature, the Noah's Ark was regarded as a suitable toy in even the strictist families. *Courtesy The Margaret Woodbury Strong Museum.*

WARSHIP, H.M.S. BLAKE c. 1890-1910; lithographed paper on jigsaw-cut stained wood; R. Bliss Manufacturing Company, Pawtucket, Rhode Island. Ships, in all materials, are among the most popular antique American toys. *Courtesy The Margaret Woodbury Strong Museum.*

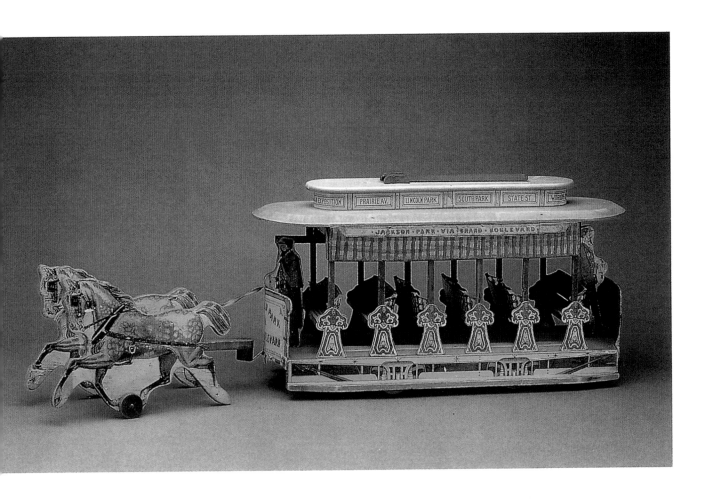

COLUMBIAN TROLLEY
c. 1893-1905; lithographed
paper over stained saw-cut wood;
R. Bliss Manufacturing Company,
Pawtucket, Rhode Island. This
pull toy first appeared in 1893,
the year of the Columbian
Exposition in Chicago. It is
similar to the trolleys which
conveyed the huge crowds
to the fair. *Courtesy The Margaret
Woodbury Strong Museum.*

NOAH'S ARK WITH PANORAMA
patented 1877; lithographed
paper on painted wood; United
States. This unusual toy features
a panoramic wheel in the door
of the ark which displays various
wild animals. *Courtesy The Margaret
Woodbury Strong Museum.*

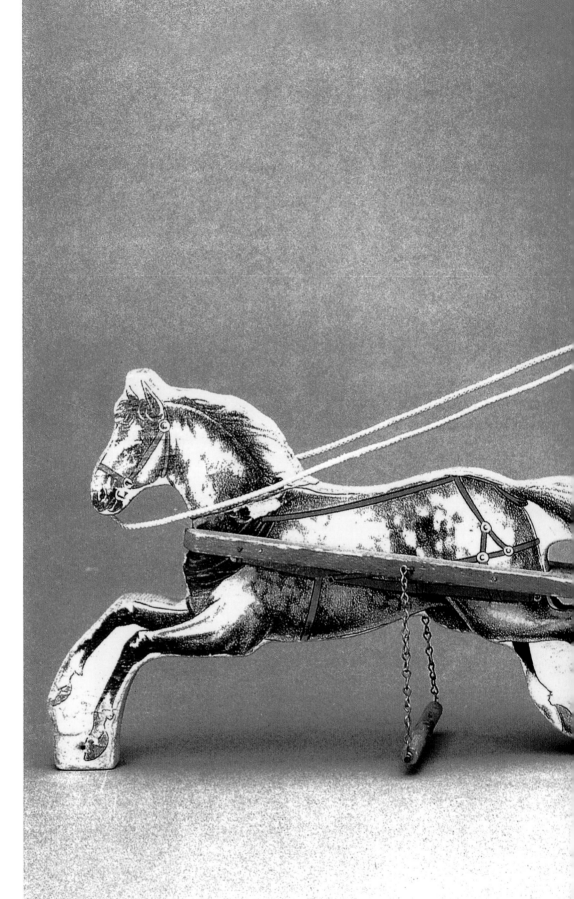

HOSE REEL WAGON
c. 1900-1910; litho-
graphed paper on
jigsaw-cut wood;
R. Bliss Manu-
facturing Company,
Pawtucket, Rhode
Island. Inexpensive
though fragile,
wooden toys have long
been popular. *Courtesy
The Margaret Wood-
bury Strong Museum.*

CARRIAGE HOUSE c. 1900-1910; lithographed paper on stained saw-cut wood and fiberboard; Germany. This attractive example of a Victorian outbuilding, was perhaps part of a set which included two or three other such structures and a large, elegant main house. *Courtesy The Margaret Woodbury Strong Museum.*

DOLLHOUSE c. 1900-1910; lithographed pape stained saw-cut wood; R. Bliss Manufacturing Com Pawtucket, Rhode Island. As in this case, folky dollhouses often mimicked current architectural st *Courtesy The Margaret Woodbury Strong Muse*

CHAPTER 8

FOLKY FABRICS: TEXTILE ART

While quilts, coverlets, and hooked rugs are often considered apart from other folk-art crafts, nevertheless they are fabrics with a distinct folk character. Indeed, if defined by the maker's intentions they are among the most folky creations of all. The famous folk painter Grandma Moses started out designing worsted pictures, a form of embroidery akin to rug hooking—and rug hookers were nothing if not creative. In *Collecting Hooked Rugs* (Century Publishing Company, New York, 1927), the authors Elizabeth Waugh and Edith Foley described the source of one such artist's inspiration

> "What is that?" one of the authors once inquired of a modern design representing what appeared to be a jellyfish with octopus-like tentacles; she was collecting rugs in Newfoundland and thought perhaps she had happened upon a rare drawing of some strange monster of the deep.
>
> "A ram" was the reply.
>
> "Ram" means tomcat in the language of Newfoundland.
>
> "But" she protested, "how did you come to draw a cat like that?"
>
> "Oh, us first catched the ram; then us held him down on the mat and us drawed around him. But he wriggled some."

But there was passion as well as humor in folk textiles. Denied access to many areas of artistic expression, women often put their creative souls into their work. As one quilter described it

> It took me more than twenty years, nearly twenty-five, I reckon, in the evening after supper when the children were all put to bed. My whole life is in that quilt. It scares me sometimes when I look at it. All my joys and all my sorrows are stitched into those little pieces... I tremble sometimes when I remember what that quilt knows about me.
>
> THE STANDARD BOOK OF QUILTMAKING AND COLLECTING,
> DOVER PUBLICATIONS, NEW YORK, 1960

ALBUM QUILT c. 1850-1860; attributed to Pennsylvania. This appliqued bed covering is composed of nine large blocks set within a rolling floral border, a characteristic Pennsylvania construction. *Private Collection.*

Quilts

Quiltmaking was for many years one of the major forms of artistic expression for American women, as well as an important social occupation. While it is generally agreed that the technique of quilting—sewing together two layers of fabric within which is often contained a third, which might be

CRIB QUILT c. 1940; pieced and appliqued cotton with "stuffed work". Eastern or Midwestern. Crib quilts are very popular with collectors as they can readily be mounted for wall display. *Courtesy Kelter-Malcé Antiques.*

anything from raw cotton to an old woolen blanket—is Asiatic in origin, it is also clear that it was in the United States that the technique was brought to its highest form of development as a bed-covering. In fact, other than for a few late-19th century English crazy quilts (thought to have been inspired by American examples), early quilts were exclusively American in origin.

There are three basic quilt types—pieced, applique, and crazy—though the elements of each may often be combined with the others. Examples of the first two categories may date in some cases as far back as the 18th century, while the crazy quilt is a late Victorian development. All might be—and usually were—assembled by an individual, working alone over a wooden quilt frame. However, the quilting bee, a social occasion when many women gathered to assemble and stitch together previously prepared quilt blocks, has become as synonymous with rural American life as the barn dance or the corn husking bee.

Pieced quilts are in a sense the embodiment of American thrift and artistic expression. In homes where nothing could be wasted, bits of fabric—usually cotton or wool from discarded garments or bed clothes—were cut into various geometric shapes and laboriously sewn together into intricate designs which were given exotic names such as Blazing Star, Nine Patch, Endless Chain, or Wandering Foot. The latter was a pattern never made for a young man's bed for fear it might inspire him to "go West" and join the great migration of the 1800s that severed families and populated the empty plains.

The completed patchwork quilt top was then joined to a backing, usually of store-bought printed fabric, but in poorer families of bleached flour sacks. An interior filling provided warmth. The term quilting actually refers to the intricate and time-consuming stitchwork which joined the three layers together. For some collectors this needlework quilting—often in floral or geometric patterns integrated into the overall design—is far more important than the spectacular and colorful pieced work. The much sought-after Amish quilts of Ohio, Indiana, and Pennsylvania in particular, often consist of large blocks of geometric patterning set in a simple though bold colorscheme with remarkably detailed quilting.

HARVEST SUN QUILT
c. 1870-1890; Southwestern United States. This pieced quilt is one of numerous variations on the popular star pattern. In Massachusetts it is called Ship's Wheel and in the Midwest, Prairie Star. *Private Collection.*

ALBUM QUILT
c. 1840-1870; pieced and appliqued fabrics with a variety of figural designs. Eastern United States, possibly Maryland. A spectacular example of the sampler quilt featuring an American sailing ship. *Private Collection.*

FOLKY FABRICS: TEXTILE ART

pplique quilts, a category much favored by collectors, are made by cutting out figural design
ments—flowers, humans, and animals for example—and sewing them to a quilt top made from
ngle piece of fabric. In the so-called album quilts a group of women often contributed a single
are each with applique figures. These were quilted together at a bee amidst neighborhood gos-
singing, and general merriment.

ince the ground for an applique quilt was usually a single piece of cloth—in early times a cost-
mported cotton or linen spread with the design elements cut from chintz or calico fabric—such
spreads tended to be more costly than the usual pieced quilt. They also were sometimes pro-
ed by professional quiltmakers who used metal or paper templates to "line out" patterns which
y or their customers completed. A good example is the category of famous Baltimore album
ts, produced in the vicinity of that city during the 1840s and 1850s.

was also quite common for quilters to combine the applique and piecing techniques, as in
um or friendship quilts, where individual appliqued squares were pieced together. Friendship
ts were often made for a local minister and contained a square made by each parishioner.

he final evolution of quilted bedcoverings, the crazy quilt, developed during the late 1880s
en well-to-do homemakers began to put together bits of silk, satin, and other costly fabrics in
dom, usually geometric, patterns enlivened by embroidery and the addition of such unexpect-
items as political party ribbons and silken pictures given away with cigars and cigarettes.

REATH QUILT 20th century;
American. This appliqued
d finely quilted bedcovering
ncorporates various religious
motifs as well as other unex-
pectedly secular ones such
as a dollar sign and a group
of bombs! Contemporary
quilters often deal with
such nontraditional themes.
Private Collection.

CED AND APPLIQUED
ILT c. 1860-1880;
tern or Midwestern.
ilting quality is very
ortant to some collectors,
this piece shows the
plexity of needlework
is highly sought after.
ate Collection.

ew crazy quilts were ever intended for a bed. They were far too fragile for such use. Made in ious odd sizes, they served as throws to drape the backs of sofas or to be spread upon pianos or les. While all quilts are fragile, silk and satin ones are particularly so. Few examples in mint dition can be found today.

Crazy quilts typically combined piecing and applique. Quilting, so important in earlier forms, s of the simplest sort taking a distinct secondary role to the elaborate embroidery executed in lti-colored silk floss. Unlike most other traditional quilt types, crazy quilts are often signed l/or dated, allowing a researcher to trace their manufacture and history.

Closely related are embroidered quilts, another turn-of-the-century development. In these bed-erings, sheets of cotton, or in rare cases woolen, fabric are covered with embroidered figures, gans, names, and dates. Not so much quilts as large pieces of needlework, these have attracted nt collector interest and remain quite inexpensive.

Quiltmaking, which appeared to be dying out in the late 1800s as inexpensive, factory-made bed-eads became widely available, has undergone a renaissance in this century. During the 1930s, eco-mic depression spurred home production of bedclothes, and since 1960 a wave of needlework ft enthusiasts has produced tens of thousands of new quilts, often in revolutionary designs that m more related to contemporary art than to traditional patterns. Collecting early examples has come an obsession for some, with rare or popular examples such as Amish and elaborate applique lts bringing prices in the tens of thousands of dollars, while seminars and shows devoted to the ft flourish. It appears that quilts and quiltmakers will be with us for many decades to come.

Following Page:
HOOKED RUG 1979;
made by Ethel Bishop,
Maine. Hooked in felt,
cotton, and wool on
burlap, this interesting
rug captures the massive
appearance of a domestic
animal. More recent rugs are
often as appealing as earlier
examples. *Private Collection.*

DIAMOND IN SQUARE QUILT c. 1900-1920;
Amish; Pennsylvania.
Powerful geometric forms
combined with sophisticated
quilting on the pieced woolen
fabric set apart the highly
desirable Amish quilts.
Private Collection.

RIP AROUND THE WORLD
UILT c. 1940; Pennsylvania.
variation of the simple
ne-patch quilt, this pieced
attern consists of hundreds
f tiny cotton fabric squares,
l sewn together. *Courtesy
elter-Malcé Antiques.*

Hooked Rugs

Another popular folk craft is rug hooking. With this relatively simple technique a design is c
ated by pulling foot-long strips of colored yarn or cut cloth through a burlap backing with a lai
needle-like tool. Loops are formed which support each other on the rug surface, while they
pulled tight against the backing to create a duplicate pattern on the reverse side of the rug. Co
variations in the fabric create the rug's design.

While one-of-a-kind patterns may be created by drawing freehand pictures on the burlap, m
hooked rugs are built on commercially printed burlap. This is ideal for the purpose, since its loc
crosshatch weave allows easy entry for the tool and fabric strips. The earliest commercial rug p
terns appeared in the mid-1800s. One of the better known fabricators was Edward Sands Frost
Biddeford, Maine who began peddling his own designs in 1868. Today, Frost patterns, includ
his well-known lion, are eagerly sought by collectors.

However, it would be a mistake to assume that the introduction of standard patterns alw
resulted in a lack of originality on the part of the rugmaker. Anyone who has examined ma
hooked rugs and mats quickly recognizes that the same pattern in different hands assumes a
ferent look. Despite manufacturers' color recommendations, makers almost always chose th
own hues, either through preference or availability. Moreover, many added their own design e
ments—a border, flowers, or other figures—to the standard format.

In some cases even today, rugmakers eschew commercial patterns for their own compositio
In the early 1900s a farm wife expressed her artistic aspirations in a letter to the newspaper, *
Rural New Yorker*

HOOKED RUG c. 1900-1920;
New York. Pictorial rugs
like this example in wool and
cotton on burlap are highly
desirable. The best examples
are, in effect, fabric folk
paintings. *Author's Collection.*

**I enjoy making my own designs. I never knew how to sing or paint or draw; no way to
express myself, only by hoeing, washing, ironing, patching, etc. and while I never hope
to accomplish anything extraordinary, I do love to plan out and execute these rugs that
are a bit of myself, a blind groping after something beautiful.**

Rugs are typically hooked on the lap or on a small frame; as a result, few are very large. Squa
round, oblong, or oval examples ranging from 14 inches square (a typical chair mat) to 3-by-5-f

are most common. Also found
long, narrow stair runners a
demi-lune forms designed i
doorways—the latter often w
the friendly "WELCOME" gre
ing. Room-size, hand-hooked c
pets are extremely rare, thou
beginning collectors may be co
fused by the large pastel-color
machine-made rugs which we
produced c. 1930-1950. The
may be useful carpeting, but th
are not true folk art.

HOOKED RUG c. 1875-19
New England. The combinat
of eagle and rabbits in this w
and cotton rug is unique, wh
the word "Blackhawk" (the na
of both an Indian Chief an
famous trotting horse) de
explanation. *Private Collecti*

Like quilts, hooked rugs are distinctly North American in origin. The earliest examples seem to have appeared in Canada or the United States around 1800, at a time when only the rich could afford imported floor coverings. But by employing scrap fabrics (often home dyed) the housewife could produce thick, warm rugs. The craft really became popular at mid-century when loose woven burlap, used to pack goods from the Orient, replaced heavy cotton or linen foundations upon which patterns had to be laboriously punched out.

Rug designs fall into three broad categories—floral, geometric, and pictorial. Floral rugs, often based on the patterns found in imported Aubusson and Savonnaire carpets, were probably the first development. They range in pattern from highly formal compositions, often featuring a central bouquet or basket of flowers surrounded by a floral border; through naturalistic renditions in the folk-art manner; to abstract designs. In the 1920s and 1930s when collectors first became interested in the field, floral rugs were preferred. Today they are considerably less popular.

Geometric rugs feature various combinations of squares, rectangles, triangles, stars, and other similar forms. They appear to have been especially popular with women who could not afford to buy commercial patterns, since one could, with a bit of thought, devise one's own pattern. The rural housewife quoted above described her technique to *Moore's Rural New Yorker*

HEARTH RUG
c. 1870-1900; Ohio.
This interesting woolen
piece is both appliqued
and embroidered with
various motifs primarily
hearts and leaves. *Courtesy
Helaine and Burton Fendelman.*

Yes, my grandmother taught me how to hook. She used to make the sea shell pattern… took an old cup plate and lay it down on the material then run around it with a piece of charcoal wood from the fire. She used to lay one over the other so the whole rug looked like shells or fish scales.

Other rug hookers employed objects such as bricks, cups, and simple templates cut from heavy cardboard to produce their design elements. As with all hooked rugs, color contrasts often determined the artistic success of any given piece. Geometric and floral elements were often combined in a single rug, as with a central diamond motif, surrounded by a floral border. Other variations included swirling Art Deco designs produced during the 1930s.

By far the most popular with contemporary collectors are pictorial rugs featuring humans, animals, village scenes, ships, trains, and early automobiles. Earlier and more primitive examples are seen as textile folk paintings and may bring auction prices in the thousands of dollars. Particularly sought are the delicate, tightly-hooked mats and rugs made at the Grenfell Mission in the Canadian Maritimes during the early 1900s. Unusual, in that they are often made from discarded silk-stocking material rather than the usual wool or cotton fabric, these rugs feature local scenes with seagulls, puffins, whales, dogsleds, and even Eskimos. Many are labeled, "Grenfell Industries, New Foundland, Labrador."

Rug hooking remains popular. Contemporay designers have incorporated synthetic fabrics and modern themes but continue to work in the time-honored manner, while collectors continue to seek out unusual and artistic examples regardless of age.

Coverlets

The term coverlet has come to be applied to heavy bedcovering
spreads which are made from a combination of cotton and w
Unlike quilts and hooked rugs, which are made without use
machinery, they are woven on looms.

There are two distinct types of coverlets. The earlier, made in
country before 1800 and still produced, are referred to as "geom
rics," reflecting the fact that the woven designs incorporate geom
ric patterns that lack curvilinear elements. Such textiles are also o
woven on narrow looms so that two pieces must be seamed toget
to make a bedspread.

The second form more popular with collectors, is the Jacquard c
erlet, which is named for a Frenchman, Joseph-Marie Jacqu
(1752-1834), who invented a device—something like a player-pi
roll—which when attached to a loom, made it possible to weave cu
ing pictorial elements. The Jacquard device was introduced in
country in the 1820s, leading to a proliferation of coverlets v
large, floral, central medallions surrounded by borders which m
feature sailing ships, rows of houses, eagles, or representation
George Washington.

Created on looms of various sizes, Jacquard coverlets may be m
of either one or two pieces. They are also found in as many as fou
five colors, unlike the geometrics which usually are of two hue
dyed cotton (typically blue) and undyed wool. Another distinction between the two is that w
the weaving of geometric coverlets was typically a home craft carried out by women, Jacqua
were made by professional male weavers, some of whom were itinerants traveling from plac
place, taking orders, and setting up their looms to do the work. One of the reasons that collect
are so fond of this form is that it is often signed and dated by the weaver and may also bear

name of the person for whom it
made—a useful genealogical te
Ultimately though, it is the w
derful, folky quality of the hur
and animal images incorpora
into Jacquard coverlets that ma
them so appealing to collectors
American folk art.

INDEX